A-Z BA

CW00338649

CONTENTS

Key to Map Pages	2-3
Large Scale City Centre	4-5
Map Pages	6-47
Guide	
Index to Streets, Towns, Villages, Hospitals etc. and Selected Places of Interest	53-72

REFERENCE

A Road	A36	Car Park (Selected)	P
Under Construction		Church or Chapel	†
Proposed		Cycleway	
B Road	B3111	Fire Station	■
Dual Carriageway		Hospital	H
One-way Street		House Numbers (Selected roads)	13 8 3
Traffic flow on A Roads is also indicated by a heavy line on the driver's left.		Information Centre	i
Restricted Access		National Grid Reference	³75
Pedestrianized Road		Park & Ride	Odd Down P+
Track / Footpath		Police Station	▲
Residential Walkway		Post Office	★
Railway	Station / Tunnel / Level Crossing / Heritage Station	Safety Camera with Speed Limit Fixed cameras and long term road works cameras. Symbols do not indicate direction	⑳
Built-up Area	MILK ST.	Toilet without facilities for the Disabled with facilities for the Disabled	▽
Local Authority Boundary		Viewpoint	
Posttown Boundary		Educational Establishment	▢
Postcode Boundary (within Posttown)		Hospital or Healthcare Building	▢
		Industrial Building	▢
Map Continuation	16	Large Scale City Centre 4	Leisure or Recreational Facility	▢
		Place of Interest	▢
		Public Building	▢
		Shopping Centre & Market	▢
		Other Selected Buildings	▢

SCALE

Large Scale Pages 4-5   1:7,920

0   ⅛   ¼ Mile

0   100   200   300   400 Metres

8 inches (20.32cm) to 1 mile   12.63 cm to 1 km

Map Pages 6-47   1:15,840

0   ¼   ½ Mile

0   250   500   750 Metres

4 inches (10.16 cm) to 1 mile   6.31 cm to 1 km

Copyright of Geographers' A-Z Map Company Limited

Fairfield Road, Borough Green, Sevenoaks, Kent TN15 8PP
Telephone: 01732 781000 (Enquiries & Trade Sales)
          01732 783422 (Retail Sales)
www.a-zmaps.co.uk
Copyright © Geographers' A-Z Map Co. Ltd.
EDITION 3 2011

Every possible care has been taken to ensure that, to the best of our knowledge, the information contained in this atlas is accurate at the date of publication. However, we cannot warrant that our work is entirely error free and whilst we would be grateful to learn of any inaccuracies, we do not accept any responsibility for loss or damage resulting from reliance on information contained within this publication.

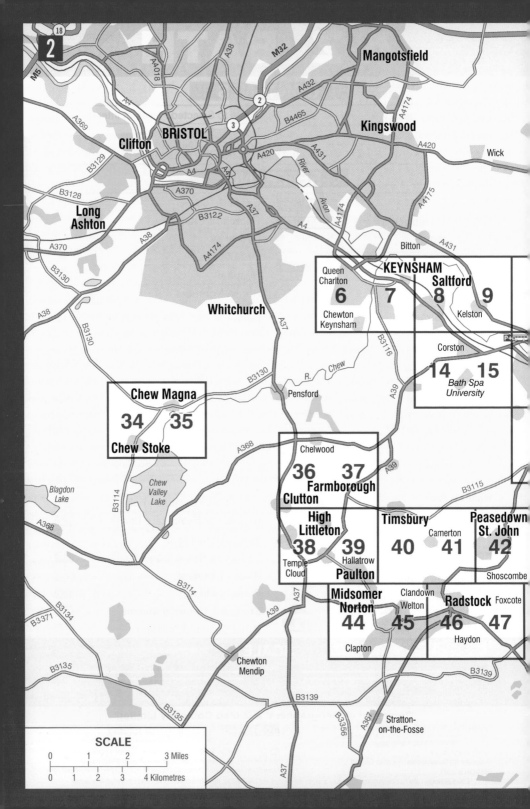

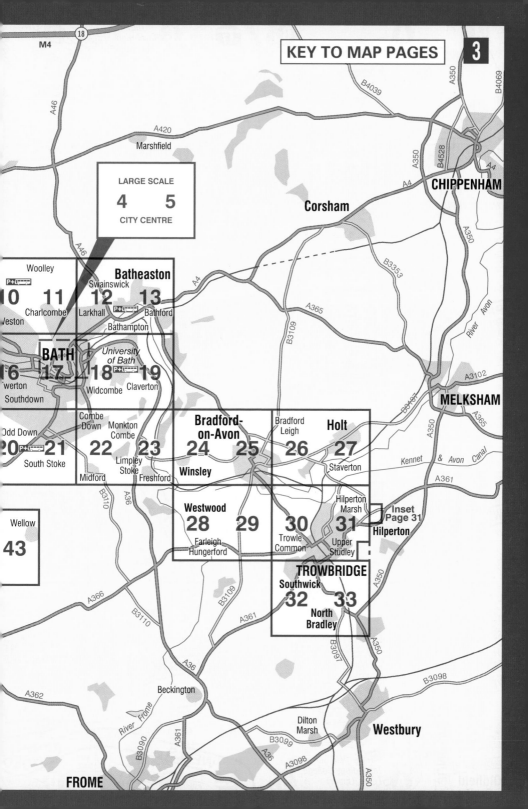

M4

18

KEY TO MAP PAGES   3

Marshfield

A420
A46

CHIPPENHAM

Corsham

LARGE SCALE
4   5
CITY CENTRE

A46

Woolley
Batheaston
Swainswick
10   11   12   13
Charlcombe Larkhall Bathford
Veston Bathampton

A4
A365
B3109
River Avon
A3102
MELKSHAM

BATH
16   17   18   19
werton University of Bath
Southdown Widcombe Claverton

Combe Down
20   21   22   23
South Stoke Monkton Combe
Odd Down Limpley Stoke Freshford
Midford

Bradford-on-Avon
24   25   26   27
Bradford Leigh **Holt**
Winsley Staverton

Kennet & Avon Canal
A361

Wellow
43

Westwood
28   29   30   31
Farleigh Hungerford Trowle Common Upper Studley
Hilperton Marsh
Inset Page 31
Hilperton

TROWBRIDGE
Southwick
32   33
North Bradley

Beckington

River Frome

Dilton Marsh
Westbury

FROME

A362 A366 B3110 B3109 A361 A36 B3099 A3098 A350 B3098 B3097 B3090 A361

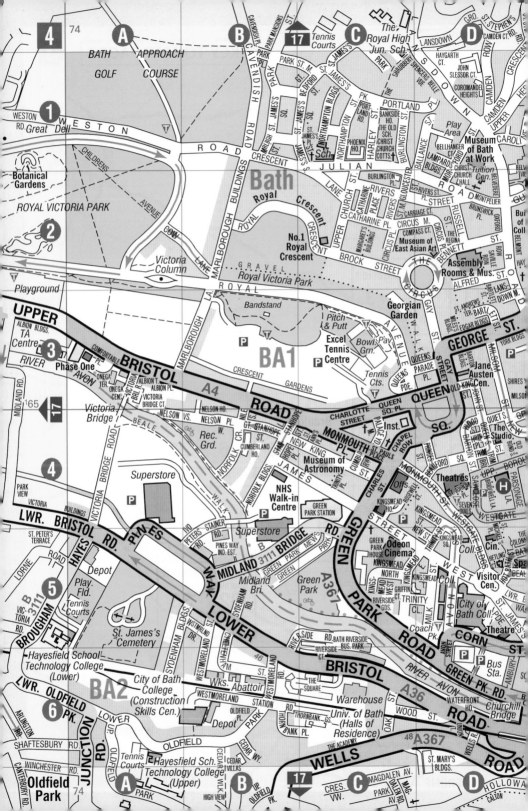

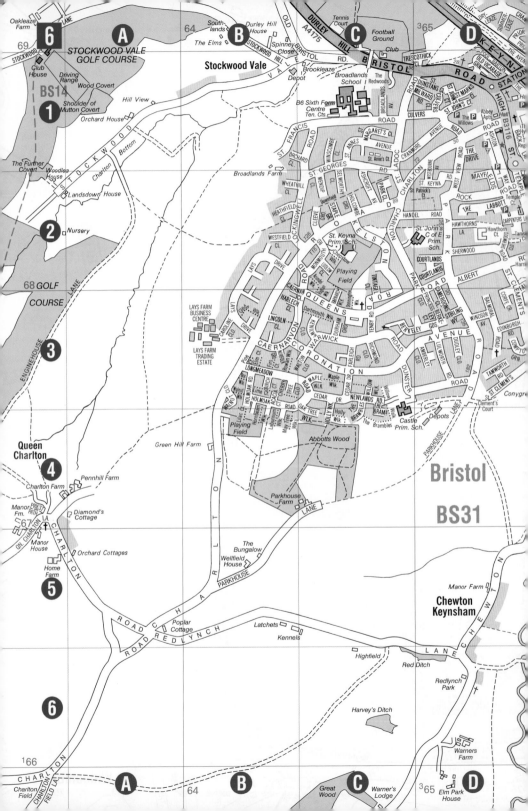

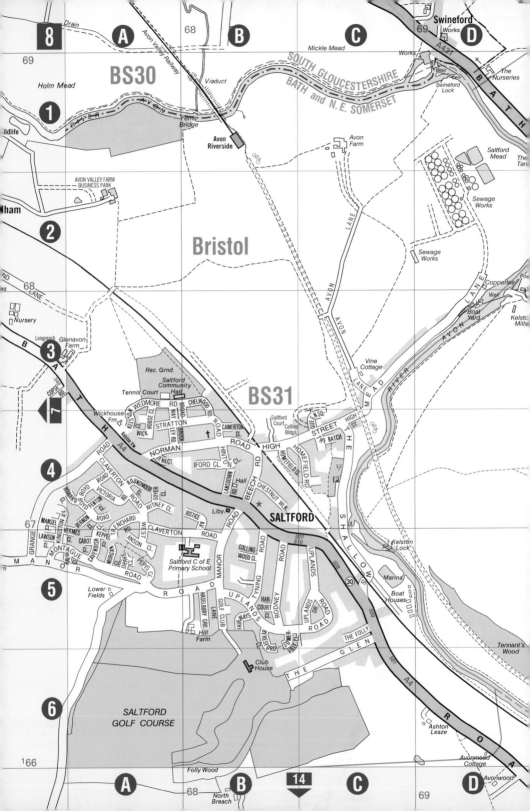

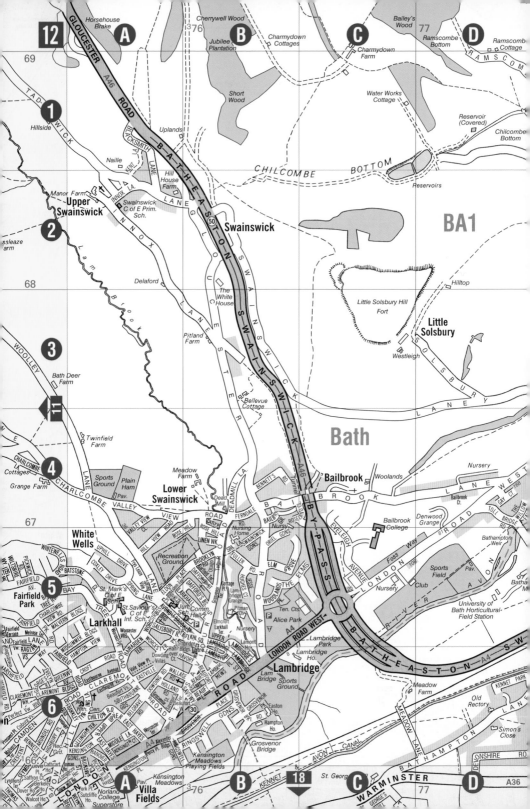

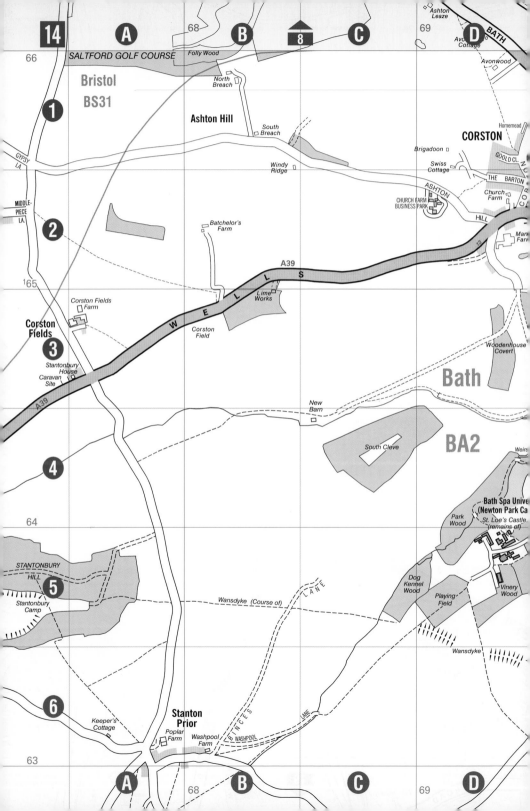

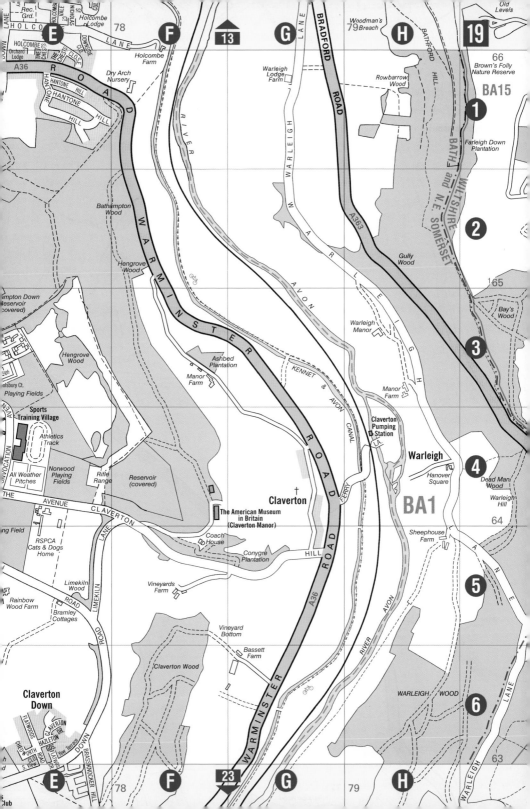

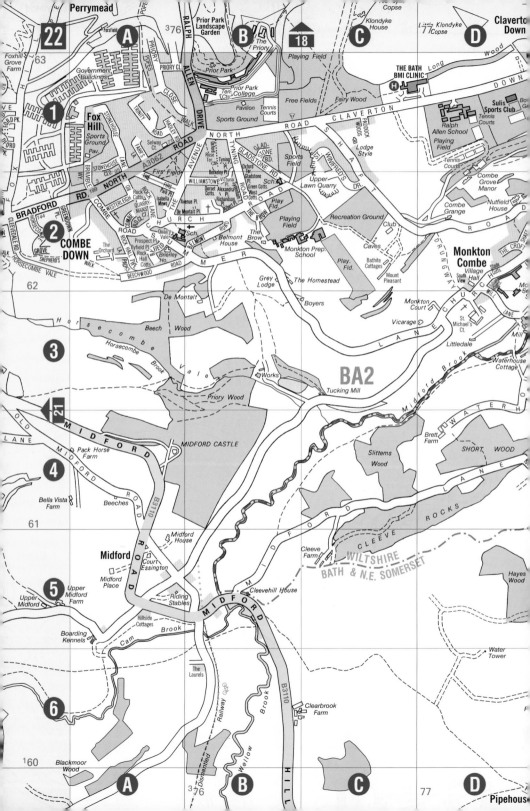

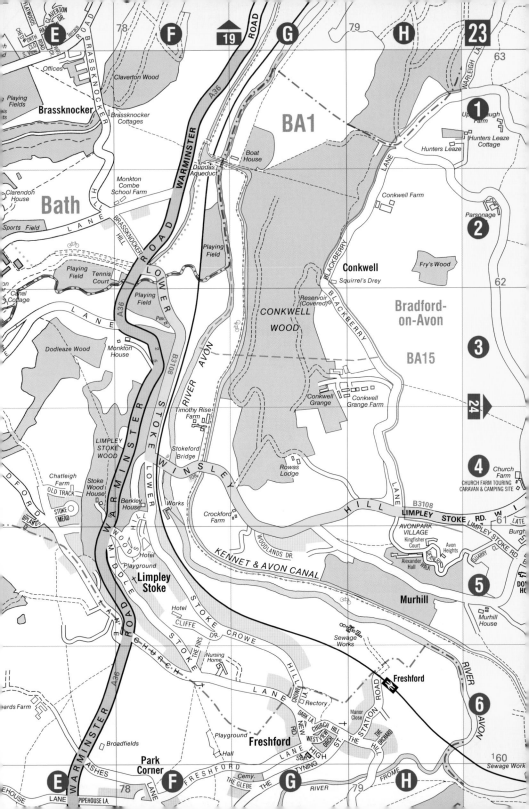

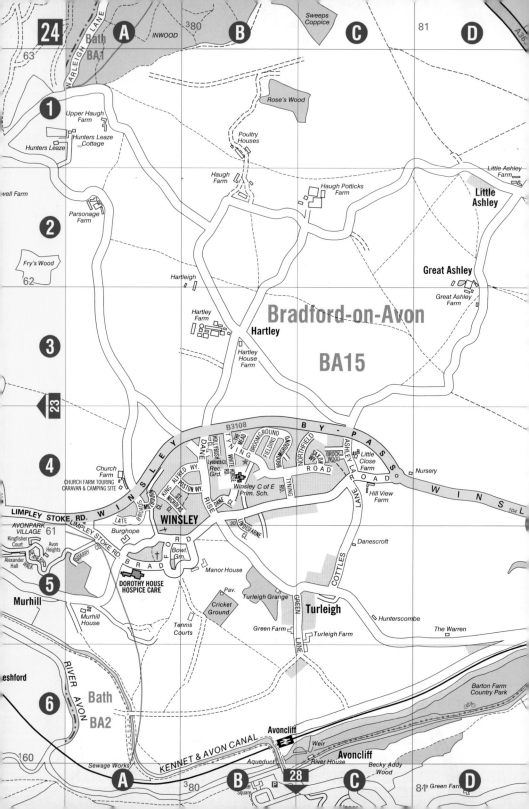

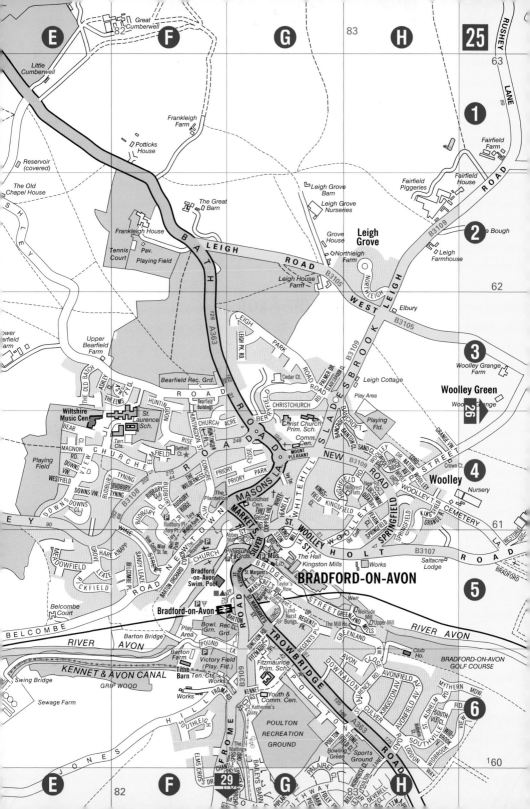

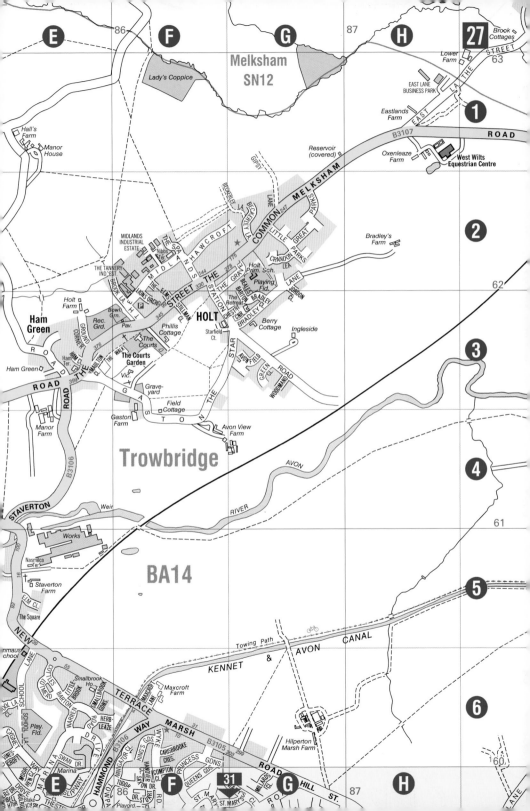

E   82 HILL   **F**   **G**   POULTON RECREATION GR   **H**   **29**

160

JONES

Bradford-on-Avon
BA15

25

The Saw Mills

ELMS CROSS DR.

CHANTLE PK

BAILEY'S BARN

SPENCER DR

Elm Cross SHOPPING CENTRE

ELM CROSS BUSINESS PARK

TREENWOOD INDUSTRIAL ESTATE

Rowden House

KENNET & AVON CANAL

BASSETTS PASTURE

PIPLAR GROUND

SOUTHWAY

FOLLY FIELD

METHUEN CL

JOHN RENNIE

Bowling Green

Sports Ground

TROWBRIDGE

Canal Farm   **1**

Marina

Southview Farm

Widbrook

Old Farm

Widbrook Bridge

ROAD   **2**

Elms Cross Vineyard

ELMS

CROSS

ROAD   FROME

Hudds Farm

WESTWOOD   LANE

59

3

30

Midway Manor

Oxstall Farm

Trowle Wood

ROAD

Trowle Manor Court Farm   **4**

58

Trowbridge

5

B3109

Trowle Farm

BA14

The Old Bakehouse

Home Farm

War Mem

ROAD   FROME

London Bridge Cottages

A366   ARNOLD'S   HILL

Arnold's Hill   **6**

MAGDALEN LA.

BRADFORD   LANE

A366

Arnold's Hill Farm

Belle Coeur Farm

Wingfield

Golf Driving Range

POMEROY

82 SHOP LA.

B3109 RD.

Church Farm

83   **H**

57

E   **F**   **G**   **H**

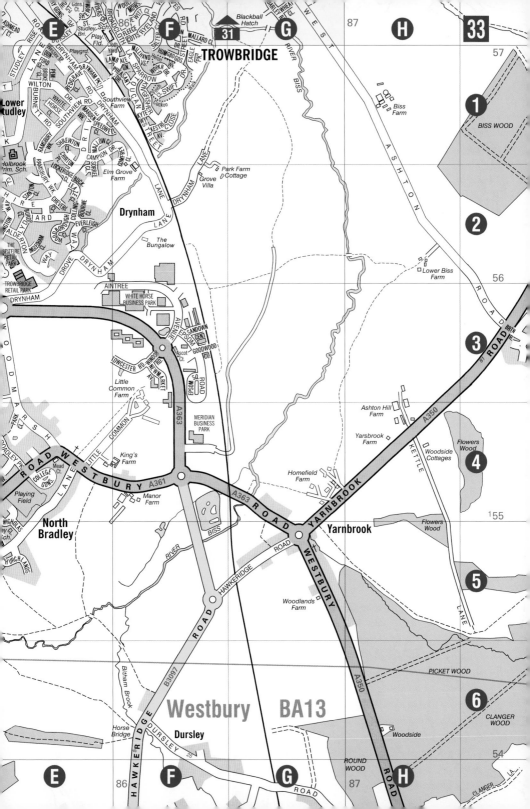

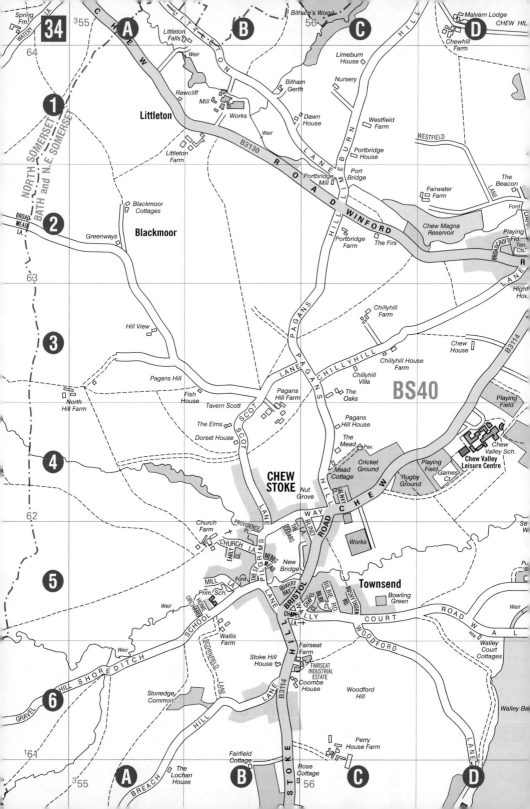

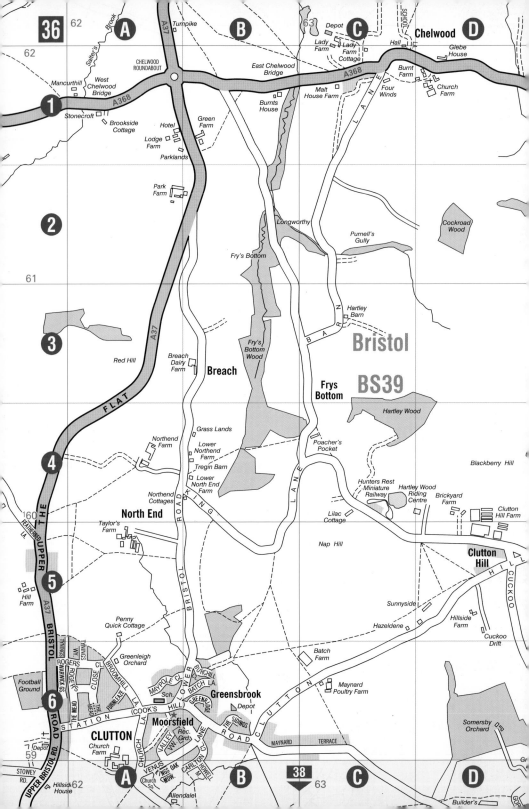

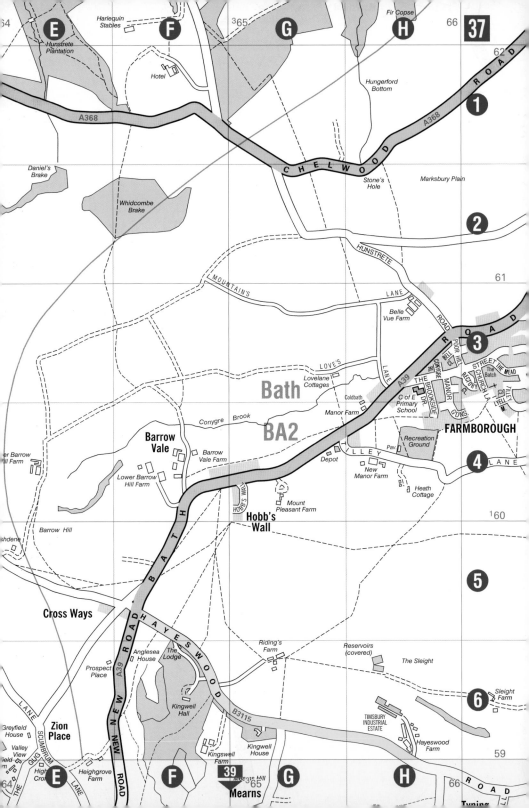

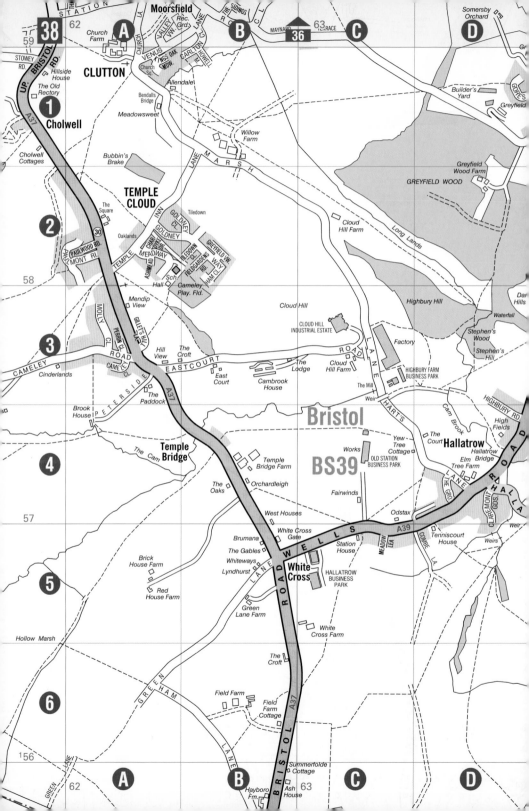

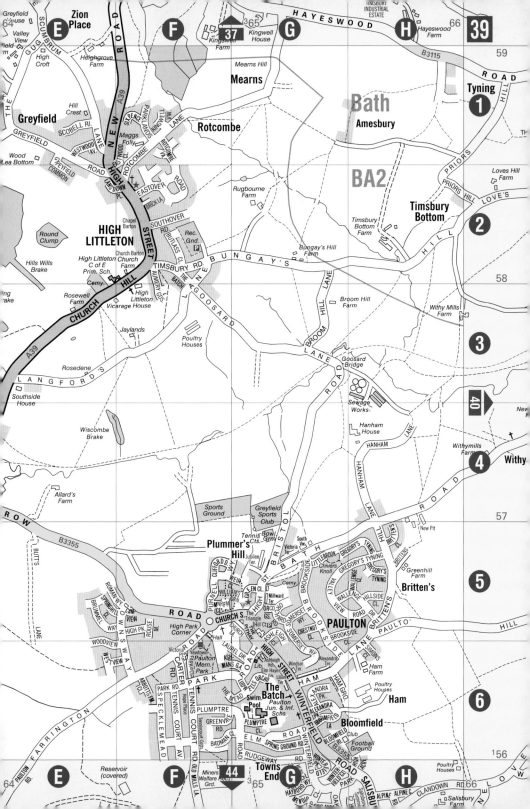

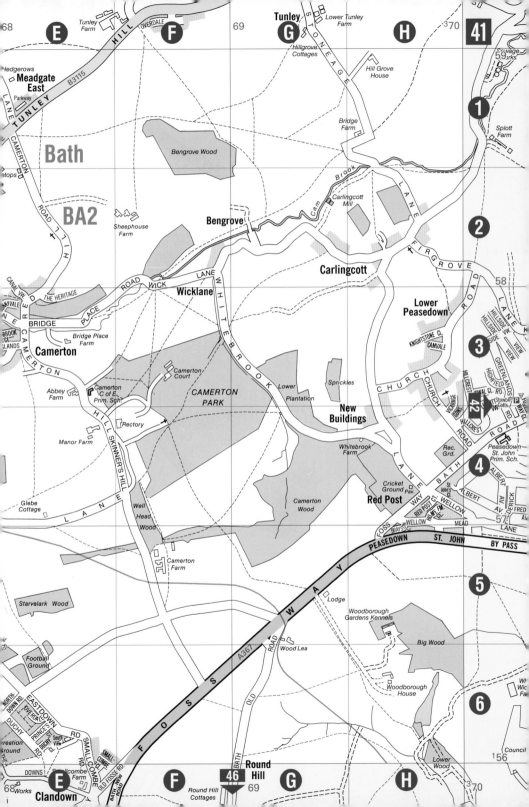

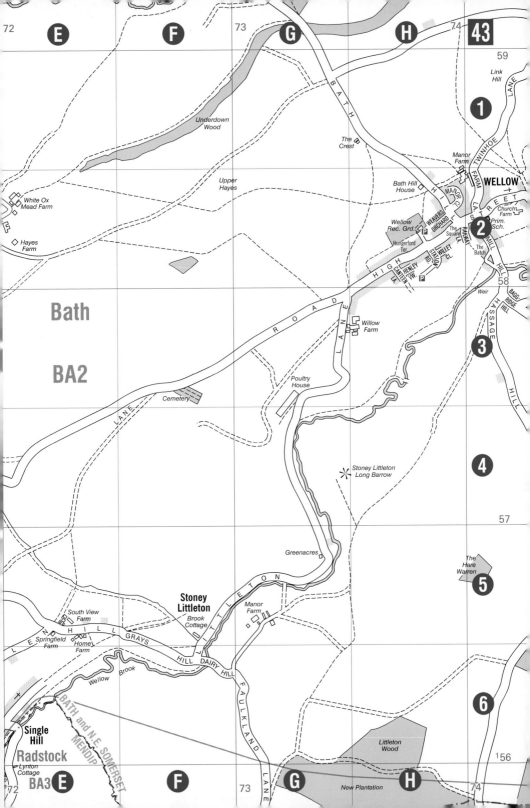

E **F** **G** **H** **43**

72 73 74 59

Link Hill

1

TWINHOE LANE

Underdown Wood

The Crest

Manor Farm

Bath Hill House

WELLOW

Church Farm

Prim. Sch.

Upper Hayes

WEAVERS ORCHARD

Wellow Rec. Grd.

Hungerford Ter.

The Square

The Batch

2

58

BAGGRIDGE HILL

White Ox Mead Farm

Hayes Farm

Weir

HASSAGE HILL

HIGH ROAD

Willow Farm

3

Bath

BA2

LANE

Cemetery

Poultry House

Stoney Littleton Long Barrow

4

57

Greenacres

The Hare Warren

5

LITTLETON

Stoney Littleton

Manor Farm

South View Farm

Springfield Farm

Home Farm

Brook Cottage

LANE

HILL

GRAYS

HILL

DAIRY HILL

FAULKLAND LANE

6

Wellow Brook

BATH and N.E. SOMERSET

MENDIP

Single Hill

Radstock

BA3 **E**

Lynton Cottage

Littleton Wood

156

F **G** **H**

New Plantation

72 73 74

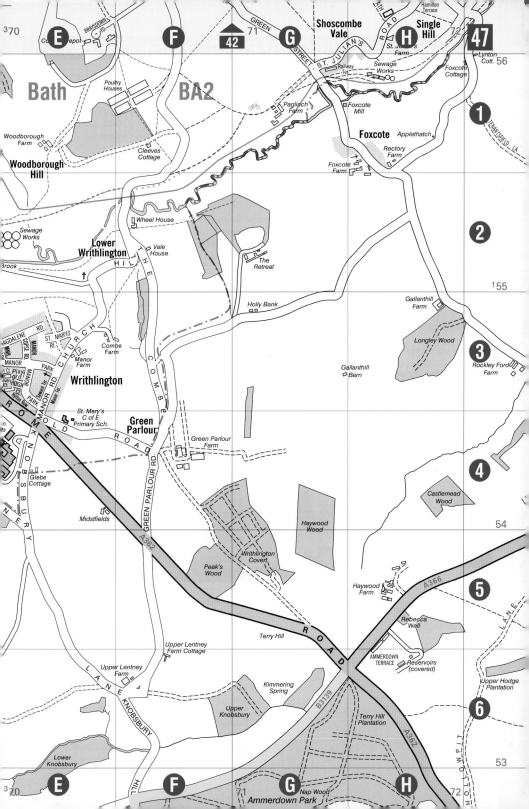

GUIDE TO SELECTED PLACES OF INTEREST

HOW TO USE THE GUIDE

Opening times for places of interest vary considerably depending on the season, day of the week or the ownership of the property. Please check opening times before starting your journey.

The index reference is to the square in which the place of interest appears. e.g. **Bath Abbey** 4E 5, is to be found in square 4E on page 5.

NT, National Trust   **EH**, English Heritage

BATH

The City of Bath is a UNESCO designated World Heritage Site rich in culture and history. This unique and diverse city is an unforgettable place to visit for the whole family.

Set above Britain's only natural hot springs, the city was first established as a spa resort by the Romans who built the impressive Roman Baths. Since then, its medieval Abbey and grand Palladian Georgian crescents have continued to attract visitors for centuries.

Today, Bath offers visitors a variety of attractions from its historic past to museums celebrating the lives of famous people who have lived there. The city has inspired and touched the lives of many through the writings of Jane Austen, artist Thomas Gainsborough and architect John Wood, three of Bath's most famous residents. Explore this beautiful city for yourself or with a guided tour. Whether it's a walking, bus or boat tour, you'll discover the unforgettable charm of Bath.

For more information visit visitbath.co.uk

© iStockphoto.com/Christian Wilkinson

© John Wallace. image from BigStockPhoto.com

Bath Abbey

Roman Baths

Festivals: In addition to the Spring Flower Show, Bath hosts several Festivals throughout the year including the International Music Festival, the Film Festival and the Literature Festival. These are staged at a variety of venues in the city.

 Tourist Information Centre

Bath (Open all year)
Abbey Chambers, Abbey Churchyard,
BATH BA1 1LY.
visitbath.co.uk
Tel: 0906 711 2000.

Assembly Rooms NT   2D 4

Bennett Street, Bath BA1 2QH.
Tel: 01225 477173.
www.nationaltrust.org.uk
Now owned by the National Trust these elegant Georgian function rooms were designed by John Wood the Younger in 1769 and fully restored after World War II bombing. It is a grade I listed building. Contains The Fashion Museum - see page 49.

Bath Abbey   4E 5

12 Kingston Buildings, Bath BA1 1LT.
Tel: 01225 422462.
www.bathabbey.org
This Grade I listed building is one of the last great
medieval Gothic churches in England. Originally
established in the 8th century by the Anglo-Saxons,
it was rebuilt in the 11th century by the Normans but
fell into ruins by the 15th century. The present Abbey,
founded in 1499, was completed in 1611 and is still
an active place of worship. Visitors can learn about
its diverse history and view items associated with the
Abbey in its museum.
Additionally, take a fully guided tour of the Abbey's
tower. Climbing the 212 steps to the top of the tower
you can enjoy a panoramic and unrivalled view of the
World Heritage City of Bath. Learn how the tower
was built, see the 10 bells and sit behind the Abbey's
clockface.

Bath Aqua Theatre of Glass   1E 5

105-107 Walcot Street, Bath BA1 5BW.
Tel: 01225 428146 / 319606.
This interactive working museum of glass brings
together the ancient skill of glassblowing and the
history of glass. Watch, learn and participate with
a professional glass blower and take home a
beautiful creation of handcrafted glass. The museum
houses collections of antique glass including Roman
Glass, Nailsea, Bristol Blue Glass and Whitefriars
Glass.

(Bath Festival Maze) Beazer Maze   4F 5

Great for picnics, relaxing and entertaining the
children, the Beazer Maze is built from local Bath
stone and set in grass, leads to a large Italian marble
mosaic of the Gorgons Head. Located in Beazer
Gardens, access to the maze can be found on the
east side of Pulteney Bridge.

Bath Postal Museum   4E 5

27 Northgate Street, Bath BA1 1AJ.
Tel: 01225 460333.
www.bathpostalmuseum.co.uk
Discover the history of post from clay mail in Egyptian
times to present day e-mail at the Bath Postal
Museum. Learn how mail has been delivered through
history and why changes were required to improve its
service. Listen to the stories of postmen and women
throughout the ages and interact with games, quizzes
and models.
Bath has been intrinsically linked with the postal
service since postmaster Thomas Moore Musgrave
posted a letter with the world's first stamp, the Penny
Black, from Bath on 2 May 1840.

Building of Bath Collection   2D 4

The Countess of Huntingdon's Chapel, The
Vineyards, Bath BA1 5NA.
Tel: 01225 333895.
www.bath-preservation-trust.org.uk
This museum celebrates the architectural history of
Bath and the people who built it. Discover through
maps, models and paintings how classical design
influenced Bath's architecture and transformed it
from a simple provincial spa into the famous
Georgian Spa City.

Circus, The   2D 4

The Circus is a trio of Georgian terrace houses of
equal length built around a central circular area.
Originally the vision of John Wood the Elder, work
began in 1754 and was completed by his son, John
Wood the Younger in 1768. It has since been
accredited grade I listed status.
Wood's inspiration came from the Roman Colosseum
by imitating its classical architecture. However, unlike
the Colosseum's spectacular exterior, Wood's wanted
people to appreciate his architecture from its inside.
Thus, each of the three terraces face one of three
entrances; so whichever way you approach the
Circus you're presented with one of the three facades
straight ahead. Famous residents have included the
artist Thomas Gainsborough at number 17 and
William Pitt (the Elder).

Fashion Museum   2D 4

Assembly Rooms, Bennett Street, Bath BA1 2QH.
Tel: 01225 477173.
www.museumofcostume.co.uk
The Bath and NE Somerset Council's Fashion
Museum, a world-class collection of historical and
contemporary dress, can be found in the Assembly
Rooms. The collection was donated to the City of
Bath in 1963 by Doris Langley Moore, a costume
designer, collector and writer.
From more than 30,000 items and through
continuous new displays, the museum demonstrates
the changing style of fashion from the 16th century to
the present day.
Collections include examples of fashionable dress for
men, women and children, accessories and fashion
photographs. A popular display is the 'Corsets and
Crinolines' where visitors can try on reproduction
clothing.

Herschel Museum of Astronomy, The   4C 4

19 New King Street, Bath BA1 2BL.
Tel: 01225 446865.
www.bath-preservation-trust.org.uk
The Herschel Museum of Astronomy is the former
home of William Herschel and his sister Caroline

Herschel who were both notable astronomers and musicians. The museum celebrates the achievements of the Herschel's who made a significant contribution to space exploration and modern science, such as the discovery of the planet Uranus in 1781. Visitors can see the workshop where Herschel designed and made his own telescopes and enjoy an audio tour.

Holburne Museum of Art 2G 5

(Closed until spring 2011 for refurbishment)
Great Pulteney Street, Bath BA2 4DB.
Tel: 01225 466669.
www.bath.ac.uk/holburne
Named after Sir William Holburne, a naval officer from Bath, the museum was founded to exhibit his personal collection of decorative art, fine art, glass, porcelain, furniture, silver and Italian bronzes. Today the museum includes works by Thomas Gainsborough, William Hoare and the Barkers of Bath, portraits by Stubbs, Ramsay, Raeburn and Zoffany and landscapes by Guardi and Turner.

© iStockphoto.com/Godrick

Pulteney Bridge

Jane Austin Centre, The 3D 4

40 Gay Street, Bath, BA1 2NT. Tel: 01225 443000.
www.janeausten.co.uk
This popular tourist attraction celebrates the life of arguably Bath's most famous resident. The Jane Austen Centre exhibits life during Bath's Regency period and how living there between 1801 and 1806 influenced Jane Austen's life and writing.
The Centre offers guided walking tours. Within a mile radius of the Centre visitors can see where Jane Austen lived and locations for her novels Persuasion and Northanger Abbey.

The Regency Tea Rooms at the Jane Austen Centre offer refreshment and views across the city of Bath.

Museum of Bath at Work 1D 4

Camden Works, Julian Road, Bath BA1 2RH.
Tel: 01225 318348.
www.bathatwork.co.uk
From manufacturing to a health resort for tourists, the museum traces 2000 years of Bath's working heritage since Roman times. It includes exact reconstructions of Victorian factories with demonstrations of working machinery.
The museum of Bath at Work also holds large collections of documents, photographs, film, sound recordings and objects connected to the historical and commercial development of the city. Audio guides and guided tours are available.

Museum of East Asian Art 2C 4

12 Bennett Street, Bath BA1 2QJ.
Tel: 01225 464640.
www.meaa.org.uk
As its title suggests this Museum houses collections from China, Japan, Korea and Southeast Asia. Exhibits date from c.5000 BC to the present day and include ceramics, jades, bronzes and bamboo carvings.

Pulteney Bridge 4E 5

Commissioned by William Pulteney and completed in 1773, Pulteney Bridge was built to connect the village of Bathwick to central Bath. Bathwick was a modest country village but Pulteney could see its commercial potential and by creating a new town and joining it directly to Bath, Pulteney could make his fortune.
Built by Robert Adam, the Scottish neoclassical architect, he took inspiration for the bridge from his visits to both Florence and Venice. It is one of only a few bridges in the world that has shops built into its full span on both sides and is surely one of the most romantic bridges in the world.
Restoration work was completed in 1951 for the Festival of Britain and again in 1975. It has been designated by English Heritage as a grade I listed building.
  Related Feature:
  Gift Shop. Pulteney Bridge Gifts,
  15-16 Pulteney Bridge, Bath BA2 4AY.
  Tel: 01225 426161.

Roman Baths 5E 5

Stall Street, Bath BA1 1LZ. Tel: 01225 477785.
www.romanbaths.co.uk
At the heart of the city is the Roman Baths with its Museum and Grand Pump Room. This major tourist attraction receives over one million visitors a year.

Take a nostalgic tour back in time and experience the opulent Roman lifestyle of magnificent treasures and social bathing for yourself. Interact with costumed 'Roman characters' and listen to their stories to bring the baths to life. In addition, children's audio tour guides are available.

Built by the Romans around Britain's only natural hot spring, the Baths include an impressive temple and bathing complex that continues to flow with mineral rich hot water at a temperature of 46°C and has been doing so for thousands of years.

Sited below the main street level there are four main areas of interest: the Sacred Spring, the Roman Temple, the Roman Bath House and the Museum. From jewellery to cooking utensils the Museum contains many diverse collections found at the Roman Baths including more than 12,000 Roman currency coins.

Related Features:

Grand Pump Room   4E 5

The Grand Pump Room is a Grade I listed building adjacent to the Roman Baths. Here visitors can drink water from the Roman Baths and eat in the restaurant while enjoying entertaining music and its neo-classical decoration.

Thermae Bath Spa   5D 4

Hot Bath Street, Bath BA1 5J.
Tel: 01225 331234. www.thermaebathspa.com
A few yards from the ancient Roman Baths is the more modern spa where Britain's only natural thermal waters can be enjoyed in a variety of over 50 treatments. Sessions must be booked in advance. There is also a visitor centre depicting the role of the spa in the city.

Inclusive ticket to all three sites; Roman Baths, Grand Pump Room and Thermae Bath Spa is available. Must be booked in advance.

Royal Victoria Park & Botanical Gardens   2A 4

Royal Victoria Park is the largest park in Bath covering 57 acres and offers entertainment for all ages. The Park was officially opened in 1830. It was the first park to be named after Princess Victoria and includes an obelisk dedicated to her. Since its creation, the Park has remained relatively unchanged, making it an important example of the Victorian style. English Heritage has registered it as a Park of National Historic Importance. The Bath Spring Flower Show is held in early May each year. Recreational facilities include: a boating pond, a bowling green, tennis courts, children's adventure playground, skateboard area, putting and a 'pitch and putt' golf course. There is also an aviary and ornamental lakes. In addition, why not take a walk through the Botanical Gardens and experience the beautiful and diverse collections of flowers and trees.

© John Wallace, image from BigStockPhoto.com

Royal Crescent

Royal Crescent   2B 4

Royal Crescent, Bath BA1 2LR.
www.royalcrescentbath.com
The Royal Crescent is a residential road of 30 houses formed in the shape of a semi-ellipse. Built between 1767-1775, these grade I listed buildings were designed by John Wood the Younger and are considered to be one of the finest examples of Georgian urban architecture in Britain. One former resident was the Duke of York, second son of George III. Most houses in the Crescent are privately owned while at the centre of the Crescent, occupying numbers 15 and 16, is The Royal Crescent Hotel.

Related Features:

No. 1 Royal Crescent   2B 4

1 Royal Crescent, Bath BA1 2LR.
Tel: 01225 428126.
www.bath-preservation-trust.org.uk
Number 1 is open to the public and is a snapshot of life in Georgian Bath. It provides visitors with an opportunity to peer through the famous Palladian façade and take a step back in time to experience aristocratic 18th century life. Each room is brought to life by tour guides and elegantly furnished with authentic furniture, paintings, textiles and carpets.

Sally Lunn's House 5E 5

4 North Parade Passage, Bath BA1 1NX.
Tel: 01225 461 634.
www.sallylunns.co.uk
Located in the oldest house in Bath, (c.1483) Sally
Lunn's House is a restaurant and museum that
combines historical cuisine and architecture.
Sally Lunn, a young French refugee, emigrated to
Bath and began work in 1680 at the refreshment
house that had been in business since Roman times.
She brought with her a recipe for a light, sweet bun.
It grew in popularity, became her trademark and a
regional speciality now known the world over.
Visitors can sample the famous Sally Lunn bun,
made to the original and still secret recipe, and other
local and historical dishes. In addition, visit the
museum to see the original kitchen used by Sally
Lunn including the Roman and Medieval foundations
of the house.

Victoria Art Gallery 4E 5

Bridge Street, Bath BA2 4AT.
Tel: 01225 477233.
www.victoriagal.org.uk
Free to the public, the Victoria Art Gallery houses
over 1,500 decorative arts treasures from paintings to
sculpture including work by Gainsborough, Barker,
Sickert and Zoffany. Exhibits include British oil
paintings from the 17th century, works by the
Impressionists and present day artists.

Other Places of Interest covered by this atlas

American Museum in Britain, The 4F 19
Claverton Manor, Bath BA2 7BD. Tel: 01225 460503.
www.americanmuseum.org
Historic Claverton Manor is home to the only museum
of Americana outside of the United States. There are
a number of period rooms from the 1680's to the
1860's and collections of folk art, textiles, quilts, silver
and glass. Originally established in 1961 to introduce
American history and culture to people in Britain and
Europe, the museum takes visitors through time from
the first settlers, Native Americans, the Civil War, to
the 20th Century. Set in an area of outstanding natural
beauty, visitors can enjoy forty acres of gardens at
Claverton Manor that have fantastic views over the
valley of the River Avon.

Beckford's Tower & Museum 3E 11
The Beckford Tower, Lansdown Road, Bath BA1 9BH.
Tel: 01225 460 705.
www.bath-preservation-trust.org.uk
Beckford Tower was built for the wealthy novelist and
art collector William Beckford in 1827. It provided him
with a study retreat and became home to part of his
library and art collection. Today, the tower includes a
museum dedicated to the life of William Beckford
containing paintings, prints and furniture.
The neo-classical tower stands 120 foot high. Visitors
can climb 154 steps to the top of the spiral staircase
and enjoy fantastic panoramic views of the World
Heritage City of Bath.

Claverton Pumping Station 4H 19
Claverton, Bath BA2 7BH. Tel: 01225 483001.
www.claverton.org
John Rennie, a Scottish civil engineer, built Claverton
Pumping Station, in 1813, to lift up water from the
River Avon into the Kennet and Avon Canal 14.6
metres (47ft) above. The pump is driven by a giant
waterwheel, which is powered by the River Avon. It
can raise 100,000 gallons of water an hour. It can be
seen working on a few days each year.
The pumping station, built from local Bath Stone, was
fully operational between 1813 and 1952. It was
restored then re-opened in 1978 and is now a grade II
listed building.

Farleigh Hungerford Castle EH 5B 28
Farleigh Hungerford, Bath BA2 7RS.
Tel: 01225 754026. www.english-heritage.org.uk
In the valley of the river Frome, approximately 9 miles
from Bath city centre, stands the ruins of Farleigh
Hungerford Castle. Originally a manor house, it was
bought by Sir Thomas Hungerford, who, between
1370-1380, redeveloped it into a castle. He added four,
60-foot high towers, large defensive walls and a moat
with a drawbridge. The Hungerford family occupied the
castle for over 300 years assuring it, and the people
who lived there, a place in English history, before it fell
into ruin.
Today, visitors can explore its remains, which include
the foundations, two towers and a chapel. Rare
medieval wall paintings and family tombs can be seen
in the chapel, while in the crypt, lay Britain's best
collection of lead coffins. Farleigh Hungerford Castle is
a grade I listed building and a Scheduled Ancient
Monument managed by English Heritage.

Westwood Manor NT 2D 28
Lower Westwood, Bradford-on-Avon BA15 2AF.
Tel: 01225 863374. www.nationaltrust.org.uk
In the village of Westwood, 2 miles southwest of
Bradford-on-Avon, is Westwood Manor, a 15th Century
Manor House with 17th Century windows and
plasterwork. A collection of furniture, tapestries and
musical instruments can also be seen.

INDEX

Including Streets, Places & Areas, Hospitals etc., Industrial Estates,
Selected Flats & Walkways, Stations and Selected Places of Interest.

HOW TO USE THIS INDEX

1. Each street name is followed by its Postcode District, then by its Locality abbreviation(s) and then by its map reference;
e.g. **Aintree Av.** BA14: Trow . . . . 3E **33** is in the BA14 Postcode District and the Trowbridge Locality and is to be found in square 3E on page **33**. The page number is shown in bold type.

2. A strict alphabetical order is followed in which Av., Rd., St., etc. (though abbreviated) are read in full and as part of the street name;
e.g. **Burnthouse Ct.** appears after **Burnt Ho. Cotts.** but before **Burnt Ho. Rd.**

3. Streets and a selection of flats and walkways that cannot be shown on the mapping, appear in the index with the thoroughfare to which they are connected shown in brackets; e.g. **Avondown Ct.** *BA14: Trow* . . . . *4E* **31** *(off Yerbury St.)*

4. Addresses that are in more than one part are referred to as not continuous.

5. Places and areas are shown in the index in **BLUE TYPE** and the map reference is to the actual map square in which the town centre or area is located and not to the place name shown on the map; e.g. **BATHEASTON** **4E 13**

6. An example of a selected place of interest is **American Mus. in Britain, The (Claverton Manor)** **4F 19**

7. An example of a station is **Avoncliff Station (Rail)** . . . . **6B 24**, also included is **Park & Ride**.
e.g. **Batheaston By-Pass (Park & Ride)** **5E 13**

8. An example of a Hospital, Walk-in Centre or Hospice is **CIRCLE BATH HOSPITAL** **5C 42**

9. Map references for entries that appear on large scale pages **4** & **5** are shown first, with small scale map references shown in brackets;
e.g. **Abbey Ct.** BA2: Bath 3G **5** (2A **18**)

GENERAL ABBREVIATIONS

App. : Approach	**Fld.** : Field	**Pde.** : Parade
Av. : Avenue	**Flds.** : Fields	**Pk.** : Park
Bri. : Bridge	**Gdns.** : Gardens	**Pas.** : Passage
Bldgs. : Buildings	**Ga.** : Gate	**Pl.** : Place
Bungs. : Bungalows	**Gt.** : Great	**Ri.** : Rise
Bus. : Business	**Grn.** : Green	**Rd.** : Road
Cvn. : Caravan	**Gro.** : Grove	**Rdbt.** : Roundabout
Cen. : Centre	**Hgts.** : Heights	**Shop.** : Shopping
Chu. : Church	**Ho.** : House	**Sth.** : South
Circ. : Circle	**Ind.** : Industrial	**Sq.** : Square
Cir. : Circus	**Info.** : Information	**Sta.** : Station
Cl. : Close	**La.** : Lane	**St.** : Street
Comn. : Common	**Lit.** : Little	**Ter.** : Terrace
Cnr. : Corner	**Lwr.** : Lower	**Trad.** : Trading
Cott. : Cottage	**Mnr.** : Manor	**Up.** : Upper
Cotts. : Cottages	**Mans.** : Mansions	**Va.** : Vale
Ct. : Court	**Mdw.** : Meadow	**Vw.** : View
Cres. : Crescent	**Mdws.** : Meadows	**Vs.** : Villas
Cft. : Croft	**M.** : Mews	**Vis.** : Visitors
Dr. : Drive	**Mt.** : Mount	**Wlk.** : Walk
E. : East	**Mus.** : Museum	**W.** : West
Ent. : Enterprise	**Nth.** : North	**Yd.** : Yard
Est. : Estate	**No.** : Number	

LOCALITY ABBREVIATIONS

Avon : **Avoncliff**	Cor : **Corston**	Lim S : **Limpley Stoke**
Bath : **Bath**	Dunk : **Dunkerton**	Lit A : **Little Ashley**
Batham : **Bathampton**	Eng : **Englishcombe**	Mark : **Marksbury**
Bathe : **Batheaston**	F'boro : **Farmborough**	Mid : **Midford**
Bathf : **Bathford**	Far G : **Farrington Gurney**	Mid N : **Midsomer Norton**
Bis S : **Bishop Sutton**	Faul : **Faulkland**	Mon C : **Monkton Combe**
Brad L : **Bradford Leigh**	Fox : **Foxcote**	New L : **Newton St Loe**
Brad A : **Bradford-on-Avon**	F'frd : **Freshford**	N Bra : **North Bradley**
B Gif : **Broughton Gifford**	Hall : **Hallatrow**	Odd D : **Odd Down**
Burn : **Burnett**	Hay : **Haydon**	Paul : **Paulton**
Came : **Cameley**	Hem : **Hemington**	Pea J : **Peasedown St John**
Cam : **Camerton**	Hey : **Heywood**	Q Char : **Queen Charlton**
Charl : **Charlcombe**	High L : **High Littleton**	Rads : **Radstock**
Chel : **Chelwood**	Hilp : **Hilperton**	Regil : **Regil**
Chew M : **Chew Magna**	Holt : **Holt**	Salt : **Saltford**
Chew S : **Chew Stoke**	Huns : **Hunstrete**	Sho : **Shockerwick**
Clan : **Clandown**	Ifo : **Iford**	Shos : **Shoscombe**
Clapt : **Clapton**	Ing : **Inglesbatch**	S'ske : **Southstoke**
C'ton : **Claverton**	Kel : **Kelston**	S'wick : **Southwick**
C'ton D : **Claverton Down**	Key : **Keynsham**	Stan D : **Stanton Drew**
Clut : **Clutton**	Kil : **Kilmersdon**	Stan P : **Stanton Prior**
C Down : **Combe Down**	L'rdge : **Langridge**	Stan W : **Stanton Wick**
C Hay : **Combe Hay**	L'dwn : **Lansdown**	Stav : **Staverton**

Ston L : **Stoney Littleton**
Stratt F : **Stratton-on-the-Fosse**
Swa : **Swainswick**
S'frd : **Swineford**
Temp C : **Temple Cloud**
Tim : **Timsbury**
Trow : **Trowbridge**
Tun : **Tunley**
Tur : **Turleigh**
Up Str : **Upper Strode**
Up Swa : **Upper Swainswick**
Warl : **Warleigh**
Wel : **Wellow**
W Ash : **West Ashton**
W'ton : **Weston**
West : **Westwood**
Winf : **Winford**
Wing : **Wingfield**
W'ley : **Winsley**
W'ly : **Woolley**
Writ : **Writhlington**
Yarn : **Yarnbrook**

A

Abbey Apartments BS31: Key .1D **6**
Abbey Chambers *BA1: Bath .5E 5* *(off York St.)*
Abbey Chu. Ho. *BA1: Bath .5D 4* *(off Westgate Bldgs.)*
Abbey Church Yd. *BA1: Bath .4E 5* *(off Stall St.)*
Abbey Cl. BS31: Key .1E **7**
Abbey Ct. BA2: Bath .3G **5** (2A **18**)
Abbeygate St. BA1: Bath .5E **5** (3H **17**)
Abbey Grn. BA1: Bath .5E **5** (3H **17**)
Abbey Mill BA15: Brad A .5G **25**
Abbey Pk. BS31: Key .1E **7**
Abbey St. *BA1: Bath .5E 5* *(off York St.)*
Abbey Vw. BA2: Bath .6H **5** (4A **18**)
BA3: Rads .2C **46**
Abbey Vw. Gdns. BA2: Bath .6G **5** (4A **18**)
Abbotts Farm Cl. BS39: Paul .6F **39**
Abingdon Gdns. BA2: Odd D .3E **21**
Abrahams Cl. BA14: Trow .6D **30**
Acacia Ct. BS31: Key .3B **6**
Acacia Cres. BA14: Trow .5C **30**
Acacia Gro. BA2: Bath .6D **16**
Acacia Rd. BA3: Rads .4A **46**
Academy, The BA2: Bath .6C **4** (4G **17**)
Acorn Mdw. BA14: Trow .1B **32**
Adams Cl. BA2: Pea J .3B **42**
Adcroft Dr. BA14: Trow .4E **31**
Adcroft St. BA14: Trow .4E **31**
Adelaide Pl. BA2: Bath .4H **5** (3A **18**)
Ainslie's Belvedere *BA1: Bath .1D 4* *(off Caroline Pl.)*
Aintree Av. BA14: Trow .3E **33**
Alastair Ct. BA14: Trow .6D **30**
Albany Cl. BA14: Trow .3G **31**
Albany Ct. BA2: Bath .3C **16**
Albany Rd. BA2: Bath .3C **16**
Albert Av. BA2: Pea J .4A **42**
Albert Mill BS31: Key .3E **7**
Albert Pl. BA2: C Down .2B **22**
Albert Rd. BA14: Trow .2G **31**
BS31: Key .2D **6**
Albert Ter. BA2: Bath .3D **16**
Albion Bldgs. BA1: Bath .3A **4** (2E **17**)
Albion Dr. BA14: Trow .5C **30**
Albion Pl. BA1: Bath .3A **4** (2F **17**)
Albion Ter. BA1: Bath .3A **4** (2F **17**)
Aldeburgh Pl. BA14: Trow .1A **32**
Alder Cl. BA14: Trow .2C **32**
Alderley Rd. BA2: Bath .5B **16**
Alder Ter. BA3: Rads .3A **46**
Alderton Way BA14: Trow .2E **33**
Alder Way BA2: Odd D .3E **21**
Aldhelm Ct. BA15: Brad A .6H **25**
Alec Ricketts Cl. BA2: Bath .4A **16**
Alexander Bldgs. BA1: Bath .6A **12**
Alexander Hall BA2: Lim S .5H **23**
Alexandra Pk. BS39: Paul .6G **39**
Alexandra Pl. BA2: C Down .2B **22**
Alexandra Rd. BA2: Bath .4H **17**
Alexandra Ter. BS39: Paul .6G **39**
Alfred St. BA1: Bath .2D **4** (2G **17**)
Allen Rd. BA14: Trow .6C **30**
All Saints Pl. BA2: C'ton D .5C **18**
All Saints Rd. BA1: Bath .1G **17**
Alma St. BA14: Trow .5F **31**
Almond Gro. BA14: Trow .2C **32**
Alpine Cl. BS39: Paul .1D **44**
Alpine Gdns. BA1: Bath .1E **5** (1H **17**)
Alpine Rd. BS39: Paul .1D **44**
Alton Pl. BA2: Bath .6E **5** (4H **17**)
Alum Cl. BA14: Trow .6F **31**
Ambares Ct. BA3: Mid N .5D **44**
Amberley Cl. BS31: Key .3D **6**
Ambleside Rd. BA2: Bath .1C **20**
Ambury BA1: Bath .6D **4** (4G **17**)
American Mus. in Britain, The (Claverton Manor) .4F **19**
Amery La. BA1: Bath .5D **4** (3H **17**)
AMESBURY .1H **39**
Ammerdown Pk. .6G **47**
Ammerdown Ter. BA3: Hem .6H **47**
Amouracre BA14: Trow .5G **31**
Ancaster Cl. BA14: Trow .4B **30**
Anchor Rd. BA1: W'ton .6C **10**
Ancliff Sq. BA15: Avon .1B **28**
Anglo Ter. BA1: Bath .1F **5**
Anson Cl. BS31: Salt .5A **8**
Applecroft BA2: Shos .5C **42**
Apsley Cl. BA1: Bath .2C **16**
BA14: Hilp .3H **31**
Apsley Rd. BA1: Bath .2B **16**
Archway St. BA2: Bath .6G **5** (4A **18**)
Arch Yd. BA14: Trow .4E **31**
Argyle St. BA2: Bath .4F **5** (3H **17**)
Argyle Ter. BA2: Bath .3D **16**
Arlington Rd. BA2: Bath .6A **4** (4E **17**)
Armes Ct. BA2: Bath .4H **17**
Arnold Noad Cnr. BA14: S'wick .4A **32**
Arnold's Hill BA14: Wing .6H **29**
Arras Cl. BA14: Trow .1D **32**
Arundel Rd. BA1: Bath .6H **11**
Arundel Wlk. BS31: Key .2C **6**
Ascension Ho. BA2: Bath .5E **17**
Ascot Ct. BA14: Trow .3F **33**
Ashcroft Av. BS31: Key .2C **6**
Ash Dr. BA14: N Bra .4D **32**
Ashes La. BA2: F'frd .6E **23**
Ashford Rd. BA2: Bath .5E **17**
ASHGROVE .3B **42**
Ash Gro. BA2: Bath .5D **16**
Ashgrove BA2: Pea J .3B **42**
Ashgrove Ct. BA2: Pea J .3B **42**
Ashleigh Cl. BS39: Paul .5G **39**
Ashleigh Gro. BA14: Trow .6D **30**
Ashleigh Ho. BS39: Paul .6G **39**
Ashley Av. BA1: Bath .2D **16**
Ashley Cl. BA15: Brad A .3E **25** (not continuous)
Ashley La. BA15: W'ley .4C **24**
Ashley Rd. BA1: Bathf .5H **13**
BA15: Brad A, Lit A .2E **25**
Ashley Ter. BA1: Bath .2D **16**
Ashmans Ga. BS39: Paul .6F **39**
Ashmans Yd. BA1: Bath .3C **16**
Ashmead BA14: Trow .1D **32**
BS39: Temp C .2A **38**
Ashmead Ct. BA14: Trow .6E **31**
Ashmead Ind. Est. BS31: Key .2G **7**
Ashmead Pk. BS31: Key .2G **7**
Ashmead Rd. BS31: Key .2G **7**
ASHTON HILL .1B **14**
Ashton Hill BA2: Cor .2D **14**
Ashton Ri. BA14: Hilp .3H **31**
Ashton Rd. BA14: Hilp .3H **31** (not continuous)
Ashton St. BA14: Trow .5F **31** (not continuous)
Ashton Way BS31: Key .1D **6**
Ash Tree Ct. BA3: Rads .4A **46**
Assembly Rooms & Fashion Mus. .2D **4** (2G **17**)
Attewell Ct. BA2: Bath .5G **17**
Audley Av. BA1: Bath .2D **16**
Audley Cl. BA1: Bath .2E **17**
Audley Gro. BA1: Bath .2D **16**
Audley Pk. Rd. BA1: Bath .1D **16**
Augusta Pl. BA1: Bath .2E **17**
Aumery Gdns. BS39: High L .2F **39**
Avenue, The BA2: C Down .2A **22**
BA2: C'ton D .4D **18** (not continuous)
BA2: Tim .1B **40**
BS31: Key .1D **6**
Avenue Pl. BA2: C Down .2A **22**
Avenue Rd. BA14: Trow .5C **30**
AVONCLIFF .1C **28**
Avoncliff Station (Rail) .6B **24**
Avon Cl. BA15: Brad A .6H **25**
BS31: Key .1E **7**
Avon Ct. BA1: Bathe .3F **13**
Avondale Bldgs. BA1: Bath .5A **12**
Avondale Ct. BA1: Bath .2C **16**
Avondale Rd. BA1: Bath .2C **16**
Avondown Ct. *BA14: Trow .4E 31* *(off Yerbury St.)*
Avondown Ho. BA2: Bath .4C **16**
Avonfield BA14: Holt .3G **27**
Avonfield Av. BA15: Brad A .6H **25**
Avon Hgts. BA2: Lim S .5H **23**
Avon La. BS31: Salt .3C **8**
Avon Mill La. BS31: Key .1E **7**
Avon Pk. BA1: Bath .2B **16**
Avon Riverside Station Avon Valley Railway .1B **8**
Avon Rd. BS31: Key .2E **7**
Avon St. BA1: Bath .6D **4** (3G **17**)
Avonvale Pl. BA1: Bathe .4E **13**
Avonvale Rd. BA14: Trow .3E **31**
Avon Valley Adventure & Wildlife Pk. .1H **7**
Avon Valley Farm Bus. Pk. BS31: Key .2A **8**
Avon Valley Railway Avon Riverside Station .1B **8**
Avon Way BA14: Trow .2E **31**
Axbridge Rd. BA2: C Down .1H **21**
Axe and Cleaver La. BA14: N Bra, S'wick .5C **32**
Axford Way BA2: Pea J .3B **42**
Ayr St. BA2: Bath .3E **17**
Azalea Dr. BA14: Trow .6B **30**

B

Back La. BS31: Key .1D **6**
Back St. BA14: Trow .4D **30**
Badman Cl. BS39: Paul .6F **39**
Badminton Gdns. BA1: Bath .1D **16**
Baggridge Hill BA2: Wel .3H **43**
BAILBROOK .4C **12**
Bailbrook Ct. BA1: Swa .4D **12**
Bailbrook Gro. BA1: Swa .4B **12**
Bailbrook La. BA1: Swa .4B **12**
Baileys Barn BA15: Brad A .1G **29**
Bainton Cl. BA15: Brad A .4H **25**
Bakers Pde. BA2: Tim .1B **40**
Ballance St. BA1: Bath .1D **4** (1G **17**)
Balmoral Rd. BA14: Trow .2C **32**
BS31: Key .3D **6**
Balustrade *BA1: Bath .6A 12* *(off London Rd.)*
Bancroft BA15: Brad A .4G **25**

Bankside Ho. BA1: Bath 1C **4**
Bannerdown Cl. BA1: Bathe 3G **13**
Bannerdown Dr. BA1: Bathe 3F **13**
Bannerdown Rd. BA1: Bathe 4F **13**
Banwell Cl. BS31: Key 5F **7**
Banwell Rd. BA2: Odd D 3E **21**
Barley Ri. BA14: Trow 6G **31**
Barnaby Cl. BA3: Mid N 3E **45**
Barnack Cl. BA14: Trow 4B **30**
Barnard Wlk. BS31: Key 3C **6**
Barnes Cl. BA14: Trow 6B **30**
Barnfield Way BA1: Bathe 3G **13**
Barn Glebe BA14: Trow 4G **31**
Barn Hill BA2: Shos 5D **42**
Barn La. BS39: Chelw 3C **36**
Barn Piece BA15: Brad A 1G **29**
Barn Way BA14: Trow 6G **31**
Barrow Rd. BA2: Odd D 2D **20**
BARROW VALE **4F 37**
Bartholomew Row BA2: Tim 1B **40**
Bartletts Ct. BA2: Bath 6F **5**
Bartlett St. BA1: Bath 3D **4** (2G **17**)
Barton, The BA2: Cor 2D **14**
Barton Bldgs. BA1: Bath 3D **4** (2G **17**)
Barton Cl. BA15: Brad A 5G **25**
Barton Ct. *BA1: Bath 4E **5***
(off Up. Borough Walls)
Barton Farm Country Pk. **6D 24**
Barton Lodge BA14: Trow 1B **32**
Barton Orchard BA15: Brad A 5F **25**
Barton St. BA1: Bath 4D **4** (3G **17**)
Bassetts Pasture BA15: Brad A 1G **29**
BATCH, THE **6G 39**
Batch, The BA1: Bathe 4E **13**
BA2: F'boro 3H **37**
BA2: Wel 2H **43**
BS31: Salt 4C **8**
BS39: High L 2F **39**
BS40: Chew M 2F **35**
Batch La. BS39: Clut 6B **36**
BATH . . . .**4E 5 (3H 17)**
Bath Abbey . . . .**4E 5 (3H 17)**
Bath Abbey Heritage Vaults ***5E 5***
(within Bath Abbey)
BATHAMPTON **6E 13**
Bathampton La. BA2: Batham 6D **12**
Bath Aqua Theatre of Glass . . . .**1E 5 (2H 17)**
BATH BMI CLINIC, THE **1C 22**
Bath Bus. Pk. BA2: Pea J 4C **42**
Bath City Farm **4C 16**
Bath City FC **3C 16**
BATHEASTON **4E 13**
Batheaston By-Pass (Park & Ride) **5E 13**
Batheaston Swainswick By-Pass
BA1: Bath, Swa, Up Swa 1A **12**
BA2: Batham 1A **12**
Bath Festival Maze, The . . . . . .**4F 5 (3H 17)**
BATHFORD **5H 13**
Bathford Hill BA1: Bathf 5G **13**
Bath Hill BA2: Wel 1G **43**
BS31: Key 1E **7**
Bathite Cotts. BA2: Mon C 2C **22**
Bath Marina & Cvn. Pk. BA1: Bath 1A **16**
Bath New Rd. BA3: Clan, Rads 1A **46**
Bath Old Rd. BA3: Rads 2B **46**
Bath Postal Mus. **4E 5**
Bath Racecourse **1B 10**
Bath Riverside Bus. Pk.
BA2: Bath 5C **4** (3G **17**)
Bath Rd. BA1: Kel, S'frd 1D **8**
BA2: Cor 2G **7**
BA2: F'boro 5F **37**
BA2: Pea J .4H **41**
BA15: Brad A 2F **25**
BS31: Key, Salt 2E **7**
BS39: Paul .5G **39**
Bath Royal Literary & Scientific Institution
. . . .**4C 4 (3G 17)**
Bath RUFC . . . .**4F 5 (3H 17)**
Bath's Original Theatre Royal & Masonic Mus.
. . . .**5E 5**
Bath Spa Station (Rail) . . . .**6F 5 (4H 17)**
Bath Spa University
Newton Pk. Campus **4D 14**
Bath Spa University College **6F 11**
Bath Sports & Leisure Cen. . . . .**4F 5 (3H 17)**
Bath St. BA1: Bath 5D **4** (3G **17**)
BATHWICK . . . .**2G 5 (2A 18)**
Bathwick Hill
BA2: Bath, C'ton D 3G **5** (3A **18**)
Bathwick Pl. BA2: Bath 3H **5** (2A **18**)
Bathwick Ri. BA2: Bath 2H **5** (1B **18**)
Bathwick St. BA2: Bath 1F **5** (1H **17**)
Bathwick Ter. BA2: Bath 4H **5**
Batstone Cl. BA1: Bath 5A **12**
Battle La. BS40: Chew M 2E **35**
Baydon Cl. BA14: Trow 2D **32**
Bay Tree Rd. BA1: Bath 5H **11**
BEACON HILL **6A 12**
Beacon Rd. BA1: Bath 6H **11**
Beales Barton BA14: Holt 2G **27**
Beale Wlk. BA2: Bath 4A **4** (3F **17**)
Bear Cl. BA15: Brad A 4E **25**
Bearfield Bldgs. BA15: Brad A 3F **25**
BEAR FLAT **5F 17**
Beatrice Way BA14: Trow 5F **31**
Beauford Sq. BA1: Bath 4D **4** (3G **17**)
Beaufort Av. BA3: Mid N 3E **45**
Beaufort E. BA1: Bath 6B **12**
Beaufort Mans. *BA14: Trow 5D **30***
(off Stallard St.)
Beaufort M. BA1: Bath 6B **12**
Beaufort Pl. BA1: Bath 6B **12**
Beaufort Vs. BA1: Bath 6A **12**
Beaufort W. BA1: Bath 6A **12**
Beau St. BA1: Bath 5D **4** (3G **17**)
Beckerley La. BA14: Holt 2F **27**
Beckford Ct. *BA2: Bath 2H **5***
(off Darlington Rd.)
Beckford Gdns. BA2: Bath 2H **5** (1A **18**)
Beckford Rd. BA2: Bath 2G **5** (2A **18**)
Beckford's Tower & Mus. **3E 11**
Beckhampton Rd. BA2: Bath 4E **17**
Beddoe Cl. BA15: Brad A 1H **29**
Bedford Ct. BA1: Bath 1F **5** (1H **17**)
Bedford St. BA1: Bath 1H **17**
Beech Av. BA2: C'ton D 4D **18**
BEECHEN CLIFF **4G 17**
Beechen Cliff Rd. BA2: Bath 4G **17**
Beechen Cliff Vs. BA2: Bath 4G **17**
Beeches, The BA2: Odd D 2E **21**
BA14: Trow 3G **31**
Beech Gro. BA2: Bath 5D **16**
BA14: Trow 1C **32**
Beech Rd. BS31: Salt 4B **8**
Beech Ter. BA3: Rads 4H **45**
Beech Vw. BA2: C'ton D 4C **18**
Beechwood Rd. BA2: C Down 2A **22**
Beehive Yd. BA1: Bath 3E **5** (2H **17**)
Belcombe Pl. BA15: Brad A 5F **25**
Belcombe Rd. BA15: Brad A 5E **25**
Belgrave Cres. BA1: Bath 1H **17**
Belgrave Pl. BA1: Bath 6H **11**
Belgrave Rd. BA1: Bath 6A **12**
Belgrave Ter. BA1: Bath 6H **11**
Bella Vista Rd. BA1: Bath 1G **17**
Bell Cl. BA2: F'boro 3H **37**
Bellefield Cres. BA14: Trow 4E **31**
Bellefield Ho. BA14: Trow 4F **31**
BELLE VUE **2F 45**
Belle Vue BA3: Mid N 2F **45**
Belle Vue Cl. BA2: Pea J 3B **42**
Bellhanger Ct. BA1: Bath 1D **4**
Bell Heather Cl. BA14: Stav 1E **31**
Bellotts Rd. BA2: Bath 3D **16**
Belmont BA1: Bath 2D **4** (2G **17**)
Belmont Rd. BA2: C Down 2B **22**
Belmore Gdns. BA2: Bath 6C **16**
Belton Ct. BA1: W'ton 5C **10**
Belton Ho. BA1: W'ton 5C **10**
Belvedere BA1: Bath 2D **4** (2G **17**)
Belvedere Pl. *BA1: Bath 1D **4***
(off Morford St.)
Belvedere Vs. BA1: Bath 1D **4** (1G **17**)
Belvoir Rd. BA2: Bath 4E **17**
Bendalls Bri. BS39: Clut 1A **38**
BENGROVE **2F 41**
Bennett's La. BA1: Bath 6H **11**
Bennett's Rd. BA1: Swa 4B **12**
Bennett St. BA1: Bath 2D **4** (2G **17**)
Beresford Cl. BS31: Salt 5B **8**
Beresford Gdns. BA1: W'ton 4B **10**
Berkeley Av. BA3: Mid N 3E **45**
Berkeley Ct. BA2: Bath 4H **5** (3B **18**)
Berkeley Gdns. BS31: Key 3C **6**
Berkeley Ho. BA1: Bath 1H **17**
Berkeley Pl. BA1: Bath 1E **5** (1H **17**)
BA2: C Down 1B **22**
Berkeley Rd. BA14: Trow 5B **30**
Berryfield Rd. BA15: Brad A 4G **25**
Bethell Ct. BA15: Brad A 4F **25**
Bewdley Rd. BA2: Bath 5A **18**
Bewley Rd. BA14: Trow 2D **32**
Bilbie Cl. BS40: Chew S 5C **34**
Bilbie Rd. BS40: Chew S 5C **34**
Bilbury Ho. BA1: W'ton 5C **10**
Bilbury La. BA1: Bath 5E **5** (3H **17**)
Binces La. BA2: Stan P 6B **14**
Bince's Lodge La.
BA3: Mid N .1E **45**
Birch Ct. BS31: Key 3B **6**
Birchenleaze BA14: N Bra 4D **32**
Birch Gdns. BA14: Hilp 6H **31**
Birch Rd. BA3: Rads 4A **46**
Bishopsmead BA14: Stav 1D **30**
Biss Mdw. BA14: Trow 5B **30**
Biss Meadows Country Pk. **6F 31**
Blackberry La. BA1: Lim S 3G **23**
BA2: Lim S 3G **23**
BA15: W'ley 2G **23**
Blackberry Way BA3: Mid N 2D **44**
Blackbird Cl. BA3: Mid N 5F **45**
BLACKMOOR **2A 34**
Blackmore Dr. BA2: Bath 4C **16**
Blacksmith La. BA1: Up Swa 1A **12**
Blacksmiths La. BA1: Kel 4E **9**
Black Swan Ct. *BA14: Trow 4E **31***
(off Adcroft St.)
Blackthorn Way BA14: Stav 1E **31**
Bladud Bldgs. BA1: Bath 3E **5** (2H **17**)
Blagdon Pk. BA2: Bath 5B **16**
Blair Rd. BA14: Trow 1B **32**
Blake Ct. BA14: Stav 1E **31**
Blease Cl. BA14: Stav 1E **31**
Blenheim Cl. BA2: Pea J 4B **42**
Blenheim Gdns. BA1: Bath 5H **11**
Blind La. BA1: W'ton 5D **10**
BA14: S'wick 5A **32**
BS40: Chew S 5C **34**
Bloomfeld Ri. BS39: Paul 6G **39**
BLOOMFIELD
BA2 . . . .**1E 21**
BS39 . . . .**6G 39**
Bloomfield Av. BA2: Bath 5F **17**
Bloomfield Cres. BA2: Bath 1E **21**
Bloomfield Dr. BA2: Odd D 1D **20**
Bloomfield Gro. BA2: Bath 6F **17**
Bloomfield La. BS39: Paul 6G **39**
Bloomfield Pk. BA2: Bath 6F **17**
Bloomfield Ri. BA2: Odd D 1E **21**
Bloomfield Ri. Nth. BA2: Odd D 1E **21**
Bloomfield Rd. BA2: Bath, Odd D 1E **21**
BA2: Tim 1B **40**
Bloomfield Tennis & Bowling Club **6F 17**
Bloomfield Ter. BA2: Pea J 4A **42**
Bluebell Ri. BA3: Mid N 2E **45**
Boat Stall La. *BA2: Bath 4E **5***
(off Grand Pde.)
Bobbin La. BA15: West 1C **28**
Bobbin Pk. BA15: West 2C **28**
Bond St. BA14: Trow 6D **30**
Bond St. Bldgs. BA14: Trow 6C **30**
Boswell Rd. BA15: West 2C **28**
Botanical Gdns.
Bath . . . .**2A 4 (2E 17)**
Boundary Cl. BA3: Mid N 6F **45**

Boundary Wlk. BA14: Trow 3C **32**
(not continuous)
Bowlditch La. BA3: Mid N 1F **45**
Boxbury Hill BS39: Paul 2C **44**
Box Rd. BA1: Bathf 4G **13**
Box Wlk. BS31: Key 3B **6**
Boyce Cl. BA2: Bath 4A **16**
Boyd Rd. BS31: Salt 4A **8**
BRADFORD LEIGH **1A 26**
BRADFORD-ON-AVON **5G 25**
Bradford-on-Avon Mus. **5G 25**
Bradford-on-Avon Station (Rail) **5F 25**
Bradford-on-Avon Swimming Pool **5F 25**
Bradford Pk. BA2: C Down 1H **21**
(not continuous)
Bradford Rd. BA1: Bathf, Warl 4G **13**
BA2: C Down 2G **21**
BA14: Holt 4C **26**
BA14: Trow 4C **30**
BA14: Wing 6F **29**
BA15: W'ley 5A **24**
Bradford Wood La. BA15: Brad A 5A **26**
Bradley Cl. BA14: Holt 3G **27**
Bradley La. BA14: Holt 3G **27**
Bradley Rd. BA14: S'wick 5B **32**
BA14: Trow 6D **30**
Brambles, The BA14: Trow 3E **31**
BS31: Key 4C **6**
(not continuous)
Bramble Way BA2: C Down 1A **22**
Bramley Cl. BA2: Pea J 4B **42**
Bramley La. BA14: Trow 6E **31**
BRASSKNOCKER **1E 23**
Brassknocker Hill
BA2: C'ton D, Mon C 6E **19**
Brassmill Ent. Cen. BA1: Bath 2B **16**
Brassmill La. BA1: Bath 1B **16**
Brassmill La. Trad. Est. BA1: Bath 2B **16**
Bratton Rd. BA14: W Ash 3H **33**
BRAYSDOWN **6B 42**
Braysdown Cl. BA2: Pea J 5H **41**
Braysdown La. BA2: Pea J 4A **42**
(not continuous)
Braysdown Yd. BA2: Pea J 6A **42**
BREACH **3B 36**
Breaches La. BS31: Key 3F **7**
Breach Hill La. BS40: Chew S 6A **34**
Breach La. BA14: S'wick 4B **32**
Breachwood Vw. BA2: Odd D 1D **20**
Brewers Baroque *BA14: Trow 4D* ***30***
(off Back St.)
Brewery Wlk. BA14: Trow 4E **31**
Briar Cl. BA3: Rads 5H **45**
Briars Ct. BA2: Bath 5B **16**
Brick La. BA14: Trow 2E **31**
BS39: High L 2F **39**
Bridewell La. BA1: Bath 4D **4** (3G **17**)
Bridge Av. BA14: Trow 5B **30**
Bridge Pl. Rd. BA2: Cam 3E **41**
Bridge Rd. BA2: Bath 4D **16**
Bridge St. BA2: Bath 4E **5** (3H **17**)
BA14: Trow 6E **31**
BA15: Brad A 5G **25**
Bridleway Cl. BA3: Mid N 5C **44**
Brinscombe La. BA2: Shos, Ston L 5D **42**
Bristol Rd. BA2: Cor, New L 1E **15**
BA3: Rads 1B **46**
BS31: Key 1C **6**
BS39: Far G, Hall 6B **38**
BS39: Paul 5G **39**
BS40: Chew S 5B **34**
Bristol Vw. BA2: Odd D 3D **20**
British Row BA14: Trow 4D **30**
BRITTENS **5H 39**
Brittens BS39: Paul 5H **39**
Britten's Cl. BS39: Paul 5H **39**
Britten's Hill BS39: Paul 5H **39**
Broadcloth La. BA14: Trow 6F **31**
Broadcloth La. E. BA14: Trow 6F **31**
Broadcroft BS40: Chew M 2D **34**
Broadlands Av. BS31: Key 1C **6**
Broadley Pk. BA14: N Bra 4E **33**
Broadmead BA14: Trow 4B **30**
Broad Mead La. BS40: Regil 2A **34**
Broadmead La. BS31: Key 2G **7**
Broadmead La. Ind. Est. BS31: Key 1G **7**
Broadmoor La. BA1: W'ton 3A **10**
Broadmoor Pk. BA1: W'ton 5C **10**
Broadmoor Va. BA1: W'ton 4B **10**
Broad Quay BA1: Bath 6D **4** (4G **17**)
Broad St. BA1: Bath 3E **5** (2H **17**)
BA14: Trow 4D **30**
Broad St. Pl. BA1: Bath 3E **5** (2H **17**)
Broadway BA2: Bath 5G **5** (3A **18**)
BS31: Salt 4A **8**
(not continuous)
Broadway Ct. BA2: Bath 6F **5** (4H **17**)
Broadway La. BA3: Rads 5B **40**
Brockley Rd. BS31: Salt 4A **8**
Brock St. BA1: Bath 2C **4** (2G **17**)
Brockwood BA15: W'ley 4C **24**
Brokerswood Rd. BA14: S'wick 6B **32**
Brompton Ho. BA2: Bath 1F **5** (2H **17**)
Brookfield Pk. BA1: W'ton 5C **10**
Brook La. BA14: Holt 2F **27**
Brookleaze Bldgs. BA1: Bath 5A **12**
Brookleaze Pl. BA1: Bath 5A **12**
Brooklyn Rd. BA1: Bath 5B **12**
Brookmead BA14: S'wick 4B **32**
Brook Rd. BA2: Bath 3E **17**
BA14: Trow 5B **30**
Brookside BS39: Paul 5G **39**
Brookside Cl. BA1: Bathe 2E **13**
BS39: Paul 5G **39**
Brookside Dr. BA2: F'boro 3H **37**
Brookside Ho. BA1: W'ton 6C **10**
Broomground BA15: W'ley 4B **24**
Broom Hill La. BS39: High L 3G **39**
Broomhill La. BS39: Clut 6A **36**
Brougham Hayes BA2: Bath 5A **4** (3E **17**)
Brougham Pl. *BA1: Bath 5B* ***12***
(off St Saviours Rd.)
Broughton Rd. BA14: Trow 2D **32**
Brow, The BA2: Bath 4C **16**
BA2: C Down 2B **22**
Brow Hill BA1: Bathe 3E **13**
Brow Hill Vs. BA1: Bathe 3E **13**
Brown's Folly Nature Reserve **1H 19**
Brown St. BA14: Trow 6E **31**
Brummel Way BS39: Paul 5E **39**
Brunel Ho. BA2: Bath 3B **16**
Brunswick Pl. BA1: Bath 2D **4** (2G **17**)
Brunswick St. BA1: Bath 6A **12**
Bruton Av. BA2: Bath 5G **17**
Bryant Av. BA3: Rads 4H **45**
Bryer Ash Bus. Pk. BA14: Trow 4D **30**
Buckleaze Cl. BA14: Trow 2E **33**
Budbury Circ. BA15: Brad A 4F **25**
Budbury Cl. BA15: Brad A 4F **25**
Budbury Pl. BA15: Brad A 4F **25**
(not continuous)
Budbury Ridge BA15: Brad A 4F **25**
Budbury Tyning BA15: Brad A 4E **25**
Building of Bath Collection **2D 4 (2G 17)**
Bull Pit BA15: Brad A 5G **25**
Bulrush Pl. BA14: Stav 1E **31**
Bumper's Batch BA2: S'ske 3H **21**
Bungay's Hill BA2: High L, Tim 2F **39**
BS39: High L 2F **39**
Burchill Cl. BS39: Clut 6B **36**
Burderop Cl. BA14: Trow 2E **33**
Burford Cl. BA2: Bath 6C **16**
Burleigh Gdns. BA1: Bath 1B **16**
Burlington Pl. BA1: Bath 2C **4**
Burlington Rd. BA3: Mid N 3G **45**
Burlington St. BA1: Bath 1C **4** (1G **17**)
Burnett Bus. Pk. BS31: Key 6G **7**
Burnett Hill BS31: Burn, Key 6F **7**
Burnett Rd. BA14: Trow 1E **33**
Burnham Rd. BA2: Bath 3D **16**
Burnt Ho. Cotts. BA2: Odd D 3D **20**
Burnthouse Ct. BA2: Odd D 3D **20**
Burnt Ho. Rd. BA2: Odd D 3E **21**
Burton St. BA1: Bath 4E **5** (3H **17**)
Bushy Coombe BA3: Mid N 2D **44**
Bushythorn Rd. BS40: Chew S 5C **34**
Butham La. BS40: Chew M 1E **35**
Butlass Cl. BS39: High L 2F **39**
Butt's La. BS39: Hall 5E **39**
Byfield BA2: C Down 2A **22**
Byfield Bldgs. *BA2: C Down 2A* ***22***
(off Byfield Pl.)
Byfield Pl. BA2: C Down 2A **22**
Byron Rd. BA2: Bath 5G **17**
Bythesea Rd. BA14: Trow 5D **30**

C

Cabot Cl. BS31: Salt 5A **8**
Cadbury Rd. BS31: Key 5F **7**
Cadby Cl. BA14: Trow 5G **31**
Cadby Ho. BA2: Bath 3B **16**
Caernarvon Cl. BS31: Key 2B **6**
Caernarvon Rd. BS31: Key 3B **6**
Caern Well Pl. BA1: Bath 1E **5**
Calder Cl. BS31: Key 3F **7**
Caledonian Rd. BA2: Bath 3E **17**
Calton Gdns. BA2: Bath 4G **17**
Calton Rd. BA2: Bath 4H **17**
Calton Wlk. BA2: Bath 6D **4** (4G **17**)
Cambridge Pl. BA2: Bath 6G **5** (4A **18**)
Cambridge Ter. BA2: Bath 4A **18**
Cam Brook Cl. BA2: Cam 3D **40**
Camden Ct. BA1: Bath 1D **4** (1G **17**)
Camden Cres. BA1: Bath 1D **4** (1G **17**)
Camden Rd. BA1: Bath 1H **17**
Camden Row BA1: Bath 1D **4** (1G **17**)
(not continuous)
Camden Ter. *BA1: Bath 1H* ***17***
(off Camden Rd.)
Cameley Cl. BS39: Temp C 3A **38**
Cameley Grn. BA2: Bath 3A **16**
Cameley Rd. BS39: Came, Temp C 3A **38**
Cameroons Cl. BS31: Key 3D **6**
CAMERTON **3E 41**
Camerton Cl. BS31: Salt 4B **8**
Camerton Hill BA2: Cam 3E **41**
Camerton Rd. BA2: Cam 1E **41**
Campion Dr. BA14: Trow 1E **33**
Camvale BA2: Pea J 3H **41**
Camview BS39: Paul 5F **39**
Canal Path BA2: Batham 5F **13**
Canal Rd. BA14: Trow 2E **31**
Canal Rd. Ind. Est. BA14: Trow 1E **31**
(not continuous)
Canal Ter. BA2: Batham 6E **13**
Canal Vw. BA2: Cam 3E **41**
Candlegrease La. *BS39: Paul 5G* ***39***
(shown as Church La.)
Canons Cl. BA2: Bath 1C **20**
Canteen La. BA2: Wel 2H **43**
Canterbury Rd. BA2: Bath 6A **4** (4E **17**)
Canton Pl. BA1: Bath 1F **5** (1H **17**)
Carders Cnr. BA14: Trow 6E **31**
Cardinal Cl. BA2: Odd D 3E **21**
Carisbrooke Cres. BA14: Trow 6F **27**
CARLINGCOTT **2G 41**
Carlingford Ter. BA3: Rads 3C **46**
Carlingford Ter. Rd.
BA3: Rads 3C **46**
Carlton Cl. BS39: Clut 1B **38**
Carlton Row BA14: Trow 1D **32**
Caroline Bldgs. BA2: Bath 6G **5** (4A **18**)
Caroline Cl. BS31: Key 3B **6**
Caroline Pl. BA1: Bath 1D **4** (1G **17**)
Carpenters Arms Yd. BA14: Trow 4E **31**
Carpenters La. BS31: Key 2D **6**
Carpenters Way BA3: Mid N 5F **45**
Carr Ho. BA2: Bath 3B **16**
Carriage Ct. BA1: Bath 2C **4**
Carrs Cl. BA2: Bath 3B **16**
Carter Rd. BS39: Paul 6F **39**
Castell Cl. BA14: Hilp 5H **31**
Castle Gdns. BA2: Bath 6F **17**
Castle Pl. BA14: Trow 5E **31**

Castle Place Leisure Cen. 5E **31**
Castle St. BA14: Trow 5E **31**
Castley Rd. BA14: Hilp 3H **31**
Catharine Pl. BA1: Bath 2C **4** (2G **17**)
Cathcart Ho. BA1: Bath 6H **11**
Catherine Way BA1: Bathe 3E **13**
Catsley Pl. BA1: Swa 4B **12**
Cautletts Cl. BA3: Mid N 5D **44**
Cavell Ct. BA14: Trow 1D **32**
Cavendish Cl. BS31: Salt 5A **8**
Cavendish Cres. BA1: Bath 1F **17**
Cavendish Dr. BA14: Trow 1A **32**
Cavendish Lodge BA1: Bath 1F **17**
Cavendish Pl. BA1: Bath 1B **4** (1F **17**)
Cavendish Rd. BA1: Bath 1B **4** (1F **17**)
Caxton Ct. BA2: Bath 3E **5** (2H **17**)
Cedar Ct. BA15: Brad A 3G **25**
Cedar Dr. BS31: Key 3C **6**
Cedar Gro. BA2: Bath 6E **17**
BA14: Trow .1C **32**
Cedars, The BS40: Chew S 5B **34**
Cedar Ter. BA3: Rads 4H **45**
Cedar Vs. BA2: Bath 6B **4** (4F **17**)
Cedar Wlk. BA2: Bath 6B **4** (4F **17**)
(not continuous)
Cedar Way BA2: Bath 6B **4** (4F **17**)
Cedric Cl. BA1: Bath 2D **16**
Cedric Rd. BA1: Bath 2D **16**
Cemetery La. BA15: Brad A 4H **25**
Centre, The BS31: Key 2D **6**
Chaffinch Dr. BA3: Mid N 5F **45**
BA14: Trow .5B **30**
Chalfield Cl. BS31: Key 5F **7**
Chalfont Cl. BA14: Trow 5B **30**
Chalks, The BS40: Chew M 2F **35**
Chandag Rd. BS31: Key 3E **7**
Chandler Cl. BA1: Bath 6C **10**
Chandlers Barton *BA14: Trow 4E **31***
(off Roundstone St.)
Chandos Bldgs. *BA1: Bath 5D **4***
(off Westgate Bldgs.)
Chandos Rd. BS31: Key 1D **6**
Chanterelle Pk. BA15: Brad A 6F **25**
Chantry Ct. BA14: S'wick 4A **32**
Chantry Gdns. BA14: S'wick 4A **32**
Chantry Mead Rd. BA2: Bath 6F **17**
Chapel Barton BS39: High L 2F **39**
Chapel Cl. BA14: S'wick 4A **32**
BS40: Chew S 5C **34**
Chapel Ct. *BA1: Bath 5D **4***
(off Westgate Bldgs.)
BA3: Clan 1A **46**
Chapel Fld. BA2: Pea J 3C **42**
Chapel La. BS40: Chew S 5B **34**
Chapel Lawns BA3: Clan 1A **46**
Chapel Rd. BA3: Clan 1A **46**
Chapel Row BA1: Bath 4C **4** (3G **17**)
BA1: Bathf 5H **13**
BA2: Batham 6E **13**
Chapel Wlk. BA2: Tim 1C **40**
Chardyke Dr. BS39: Temp C 2A **38**
CHARLCOMBE **4G 11**
Charlcombe La. BA1: Bath, Charl 5G **11**
Charlcombe Ri. BA1: Bath 5G **11**
Charlcombe Vw. Rd. BA1: Bath 5H **11**
Charlcombe Way BA1: Bath 5G **11**
Charles St. BA1: Bath 4C **4** (3G **17**)
BA14: Trow .4D **30**
Charlotte Ct. BA14: Trow 4E **31**
Charlotte Pl. BA2: Pea J 4A **42**
Charlotte Sq. BA14: Trow 4E **31**
Charlotte St. BA1: Bath 4C **4** (3G **17**)
BA14: Trow .4E **31**
CHARLTON **6H 45**
Charlton Bldgs. BA2: Bath 3D **16**
Charlton Fld. La. BS31: Q Char 6A **6**
Charlton La. BA3: Mid N 6G **45**
Charlton Pk. BA3: Mid N 6F **45**
BS31: Key 2C **6**
Charlton Rd. BA3: Mid N 5E **45**
BS31: Key, Q Char 6A **6**
BS31: Q Char, Key 5A **6**
Charmouth Rd. BA1: Bath 2C **16**
Charnwood Rd. BA14: Trow 4A **30**
Chatham Pk. BA2: Bath 3B **18**
Chatham Row BA1: Bath 2E **5** (2H **17**)
Chaucer Rd. BA2: Bath 5G **17**
BA3: Rads 5F **45**
Cheap St. BA1: Bath 4E **5** (3H **17**)
Chedworth Cl. BA2: C'ton D 6E **19**
Chelmer Gro. BS31: Key 3E **7**
Chelscombe BA1: W'ton 6C **10**
Chelsea Cl. BS31: Key 2F **7**
Chelsea Ho. *BA1: Bath 1H **17***
(off London Rd.)
Chelsea Rd. BA1: Bath 2D **16**
Cheltenham St. BA2: Bath 5B **4** (4F **17**)
CHELWOOD **1C 36**
Chelwood Dr. BA2: Odd D 2E **21**
Chelwood Rd. BA2: Huns, Mark 2G **37**
BS31: Salt 3B **8**
Chelwood Rdbt. BS39: Chelw 1A **36**
Chepston Pl. BA14: Trow 4A **30**
Chepstow Wlk. BS31: Key 2C **6**
Cherry Gdns. BA14: Hilp 2H **31**
BA14: Trow .6E **31**
(not continuous)
Cherry Gdns. Ct. BA14: Trow 6E **31**
Cherry Tree Cl. BA3: Rads 4A **46**
BS31: Key 3B **6**
Cherwell Rd. BS31: Key 3F **7**
Chesterfield Ho. BA3: Mid N 4F **45**
Chestertons, The BA2: Batham 1E **19**
(not continuous)
Chestnut Cl. BA3: Rads 4A **46**
BS39: Paul .5G **39**
Chestnut Cnr. BA14: Holt 3G **27**
Chestnut Gro. BA2: Bath 5D **16**
BA14: Trow .1C **32**
BA15: West .1C **28**
Chestnut Wlk. BS31: Salt 4B **8**
Cheverell Cl. BA14: Trow 2E **33**
Cheviot Cl. BA14: Trow 6F **31**
Chew Hill BS40: Chew M 1E **35**
Chew La. BS40: Chew M, Chew S 4C **34**
CHEW MAGNA **2F 35**
Chew Rd. BS40: Chew M, Winf 1A **34**
CHEW STOKE **5B 34**
Chew St. BS40: Chew M 2E **35**
CHEWTON KEYNSHAM **5D 6**
Chewton Rd. BS31: Key 5D **6**
Chew Valley Lake Info. Cen. 6E **35**
Chew Valley Leisure Cen. 4D **34**
Chichester Pl. BA3: Rads 3C **46**
Chilcompton Rd. BA3: Mid N 6C **44**
Childrens Av. BA1: Bath 1A **4** (1F **17**)
Chillyhill La. BS40: Chew M, Chew S . . .3C **34**
Chilmark Rd. BA14: Trow 4B **30**
Chilton Rd. BA1: Bath 6A **12**
Chirton Pl. BA14: Trow 1E **33**
CHOLWELL **1A 38**
Christ Church Cotts. BA1: Bath 1C **4**
Christchurch Hall BA1: Bath 1D **4**
Christchurch Rd. BA15: Brad A 3G **25**
Christin Ct. BA14: Trow 5B **30**
Church Acre BA15: Brad A 4F **25**
Church Barton BS39: High L 2F **39**
Church Cl. BA1: Bathf 5G **13**
BA2: Batham 5E **13**
Church Ct. BA3: Mid N 4E **45**
Churches BA15: Brad A 4E **25**
Church Farm Bus. Pk. BA2: Cor 2D **14**
Church Farm Touring Cvn. & Camping Site
BA15: W'ley 4A **24**
Church Flds. BA14: Trow 2B **32**
Church Hill BA2: F'frd 6G **23**
BA2: Tim 1B **40**
BA3: Writ 3E **47**
BS39: High L 3E **39**
Churchlands BA14: N Bra 5E **33**
Church La. BA1: Bathe 3E **13**
BA2: Bath 5B **18**
BA2: F'boro .3H **37**
BA2: F'frd, Lim S 5F **23**
Church La. BA2: Mon C 3D **22**
BA2: Tim 1B **40**
BA3: Mid N .4E **45**
BA14: N Bra 5D **32**
BA14: Trow .2B **32**
BS39: Clut 6A **36**
BS39: Paul .5G **39**
BS40: Chew S 5B **34**
Church Rd. BA1: W'ton 6D **10**
BA2: C Down 2A **22**
BA2: Pea J .3H **41**
Church Sq. BA3: Mid N 4E **45**
BS39: Clut 1A **38**
Church St. *BA1: Bath 5E **5***
(off York St.)
BA1: Bathf 5G **13**
BA1: W'ly 1G **11**
BA1: W'ton .6C **10**
BA2: Bath 5A **18**
BA3: Rads 3B **46**
BA14: Hilp .2H **31**
BA14: S'wick 4A **32**
BA14: Trow .4E **31**
BA15: Brad A 5F **25**
BS39: Paul .5F **39**
Church Wlk. BA14: Trow 4E **31**
Cinder Path, The BA2: Shos 6C **42**
Circle, The BA2: Bath 6C **16**
CIRCLE BATH HOSPITAL 5C **42**
Circus, The BA1: Bath 2D **4** (2G **17**)
Circus M. BA1: Bath 2C **4** (2G **17**)
Circus Pl. BA1: Bath 2C **4** (2G **17**)
(not continuous)
City Vw. BA1: Bath 1E **5**
CLANDOWN **1A 46**
Clandown Rd. BS39: Paul 1D **44**
Clanger La. BA14: Hey 6H **33**
Clan Ho. BA2: Bath 2H **5** (2A **18**)
CLAPTON **6A 44**
Clapton Rd. BA3: Clapt, Mid N 5A **44**
Clara Cross La. BA2: Odd D 2F **21**
Clare Gdns. BA2: Odd D 2E **21**
Claremont Bldgs. BA1: Bath 6H **11**
Claremont Gdns. BS39: Hall 4D **38**
Claremont Rd. BA1: Bath 6A **12**
Claremont Ter. *BA1: Bath 6A **12***
(off Camden Rd.)
Claremont Vs. *BA1: Bath 6H **11***
(off Camden Rd.)
Claremont Wlk. BA1: Bath 6H **11**
Clarence Pl. BA1: Bath 2C **16**
Clarence Rd. BA14: Trow 5G **31**
Clarence St. BA1: Bath 1F **5** (1H **17**)
Clarence Ter. BA2: C'ton D 5C **18**
Clarendon Av. BA14: Trow 5F **31**
Clarendon Rd. BA2: Bath 4A **18**
BA14: Trow .5F **31**
Clarendon Vs. BA2: Bath 4A **18**
Clark's Pl. BA14: Trow 5F **31**
Clarks Way BA2: Odd D 1D **20**
Claude Av. BA2: Bath 4D **16**
Claude Ter. BA2: Bath 4D **16**
Claude Va. BA2: Bath 4D **16**
CLAVERTON **4G 19**
Claverton Bldgs. BA2: Bath 6F **5**
Claverton Ct. BA2: C'ton D 5D **18**
CLAVERTON DOWN **6E 19**
Claverton Down Rd.
BA2: C'ton D, C Down 4D **18**
Claverton Dr. BA2: C'ton D 6E **19**
Claverton Hill BA2: C'ton, C'ton D 4E **19**
Claverton Pumping Station 4H **19**
Claverton Rd. BS31: Salt 4A **8**
Claverton Rd. W. BS31: Salt 4A **8**
Claverton St. BA2: Bath 6E **5** (4H **17**)
CLAYS END **4G 15**
Cleevedale Rd. BA2: C Down 2H **21**
Cleeve Grn. BA2: Bath 3A **16**
Cleeve Gro. BS31: Key 2C **6**
Clevedon Rd. BA3: Mid N 3E **45**
Cleveland Cotts. BA1: Bath 1E **5**
Cleveland Ct. BA2: Bath 5H **5** (3B **18**)

Cleveland Gdns. BA14: Trow 3F **31**
Cleveland Pl. BA1: Bath 1F **5** (1H **17**)
Cleveland Pl. E. BA1: Bath 1F **5**
Cleveland Pl. W. BA1: Bath 1F **5**
Cleveland Reach BA1: Bath 1F **5** (1H **17**)
Cleveland Row BA2: Bath 1H **5** (1A **18**)
Cleveland Ter. *BA1: Bath 1E 5*
(off London Rd.)
Cleveland Wlk. BA2: Bath 5H **5** (3B **18**)
Cliffe Dr. BA2: Lim S 5F **23**
Clifford Dr. BS39: Paul 5F **39**
Clipsham Ri. BA14: Trow 4B **30**
Cloford Cl. BA14: Trow 4B **30**
Clothier Leaze BA14: Trow 6E **31**
Cloth Yd. BA14: Trow 6E **31**
Cloud Hill Ind. Est. BS39: Temp C 3C **38**
Clover Cl. BS39: Paul 1D **44**
CLUTTON 6A 36
CLUTTON HILL 5D 36
Clutton Hill BS39: Clut 6B **36**
Clyde Av. BS31: Key 3E **7**
Clyde Gdns. BA2: Bath 3C **16**
Clydesdale Cl. BA14: Trow 2D **32**
Coach Rd. BA15: Brad A 5F **25**
Coalpit Rd. BA1: Bathe 3F **13**
Cobblers Way BA3: Mid N 5G **45**
Coburg Vs. BA1: Bath 6H **11**
Cockhill BA14: Trow 4B **30**
Cock Hill Ho. Ct. BA14: Trow 4B **30**
Colbourne Rd. BA2: Odd D 2E **21**
Coldbath BA2: F'boro 3H **37**
College Gdns. BA14: N Bra 4E **33**
College Rd. BA1: L'dwn, Bath 5F **11**
BA14: Trow 1B **32**
College Vw. BA1: Bath 6H **11**
Collier Cl. BA2: Cam 3D **40**
Collier's La. BA1: Charl 3F **11**
Colliers Ri. BA3: Rads 2C **46**
Colliers Way BA3: Hay 5B **46**
Collingbourne Cl. BA14: Trow 2E **33**
Collingwood Cl. BS31: Salt 5B **8**
Collins Bldgs. BS31: Salt 4B **8**
Colne Grn. BS31: Key 3F **7**
Colonnades, The BA1: Bath 5D **4**
Combe, The BA3: Writ 2F **47**
COMBE DOWN 2A 22
Combe Gro. BA1: Bath 1C **16**
COMBE HAY 6D 20
Combe Hay La. BA2: C Hay, Odd D 5C **20**
Combe La. BS39: Hall 5D **38**
Combe Pk. BA1: Bath 2D **16**
Combe Rd. BA2: C Down 2A **22**
Combe Rd. Cl. BA2: C Down 2A **22**
Combe Royal Cres. BA2: C'ton D 4C **18**
Combeside BA2: Bath 6H **17**
Comfortable Pl. BA1: Bath 3A **4** (2F **17**)
Comfrey Cl. BA14: Trow 1F **33**
Common, The BA14: Holt 2F **27**
Compass Ct. BA1: Bath 2C **4**
Compton Cl. BA14: Trow 1F **31**
Compton Grn. BS31: Key 3D **6**
Concord Cl. BA14: S'wick 3A **32**
Conigre BA14: Trow 4D **30**
(not continuous)
Conigre Hill BA15: Brad A 4F **25**
Conigre Sq. BA14: Trow 4D **30**
Coniston Rd. BA14: Trow 3F **31**
CONKERLL 2G 23
Connaught Mans. BA2: Bath 3F **5** (2H **17**)
Connection Rd. BA2: Bath 3B **16**
Constable Cl. BS31: Key 1E **7**
Convocation Av. BA2: C'ton D 4E **19**
Conway Grn. BS31: Key 4F **7**
Conygre Grn. BA2: Tim 1B **40**
Conygre Ri. BA2: F'boro 3H **37**
Cook's Hill BS39: Clut 6A **36**
Coombend BA3: Clan, Rads 1A **46**
Coombend Ho. *BA3: Rads 2B 46*
(off Coombend)
Coombend Ri. BA3: Rads 2B **46**
Coombe Orchard *BA3: Rads 2B 46*
(off Combend)
Copper Beeches BA14: Hilp 2H **31**
Coppice Hill BA15: Brad A 4G **25**
Copseland BA2: C'ton D 4C **18**
Copse Rd. BS31: Salt 3H **7**
Corbin Rd. BA14: Hilp, Trow 4G **31**
Corfe Cres. BS31: Key 3D **6**
Corinthian Cl. BA14: S'wick 4A **32**
Cork Pl. *BA1: Bath 2E 17*
(off Cork St.)
Cork St. BA1: Bath 2E **17**
Cork Ter. BA1: Bath 2E **17**
Cornbrash Ri. BA14: Hilp 5H **31**
Corn St. BA1: Bath 5D **4** (3G **17**)
Coromandel Hgts. BA1: Bath 1D **4**
Coronation Av. BA2: Bath 6D **16**
BA15: Brad A 4H **25**
BS31: Key 3C **6**
Coronation Cotts. BA1: Bathe 4E **13**
Coronation Rd. BA1: Bath 2E **17**
Coronation St. BA14: Trow 6E **31**
Coronation Vs. BA3: Rads 2C **46**
Corridor, The BA1: Bath 4E **5** (3H **17**)
CORSTON 2E 15
Corston Dr. BA2: New L 3E **15**
CORSTON FIELDS 3A 14
Corston La. BA2: Cor 2D **14**
Corston Vw. BA2: Odd D 1D **20**
Cotswold Rd. BA2: Bath 5E **17**
Cotswold Vw. BA2: Bath 4C **16**
Cottage Pl. BA1: Bath 5B **12**
Cottles Barton BA14: Stav 6E **27**
Cottles La. BA15: Tur 5C **24**
Cotton Mead BA2: Cor 2E **15**
County Bri. BA3: Rads 3B **46**
County Court
Bath 4G 5 (3A 18)
Trowbridge 5D 30
County Ga. BA14: Trow 6E **31**
County Way BA14: Trow 6D **30**
Courtenay Rd. BS31: Key, Salt 5F **7**
Court Gdns. BA1: Bathe 3F **13**
Courtlands BS31: Key 2D **6**
Court La. BA1: Bathf 5G **13**
Courtmead BA2: S'ske 4G **21**
Courts Garden, The 3F 27
Court St. BA14: Trow 5E **31**
Cow La. BA1: Bath 2A **4** (2F **17**)
Coxley Dr. BA1: Bath 5A **12**
Coxwynne Cl. BA3: Mid N 5G **45**
Crandale Rd. BA2: Bath 4E **17**
Crandon Lea BA14: Holt 2G **27**
Cranhill Rd. BA1: W'ton 1E **17**
Cranleigh BA2: S'ske 3G **21**
Cranmore Av. BS31: Key 1C **6**
Cranmore Cl. BA14: Trow 4B **30**
Cranmore Pl. BA2: Odd D 3E **21**
Cranwells Pk. BA1: W'ton 1E **17**
Crawley Cres. BA14: Trow 5B **30**
Crawl La. BA3: Mid N 1F **45**
Crescent, The BS40: Chew M 2F **35**
Crescent Gdns. BA1: Bath 3B **4** (2F **17**)
Crescent La. BA1: Bath 1B **4** (1F **17**)
Crescent Office Pk. BA2: Bath 1D **20**
Crescent Pl. M. BA2: Odd D 2E **21**
Crescent Vw. BA2: Bath 6C **4** (4G **17**)
Cresswell Dr. BA14: Hilp 6H **31**
Crickback La. BS40: Chew M 2E **35**
Crockbarton BA2: Tim 1B **40**
CROCOMBE 1C 40
Crocombe La. BA2: Tim 1C **40**
Croft, The BA2: Mon C 2D **22**
BA14: Trow 1D **32**
Croft Rd. BA1: Bath 6A **12**
Cross St. BA14: Trow 4E **31**
Crossway La. BA3: Clapt 6A **44**
CROSS WAYS 5E 37
Crossways La. BA2: Dunk 5A **20**
Crossways Pk. BA2: Dunk 6A **20**
Crowe Hill BA2: F'frd, Lim S 5G **23**
Crowe La. BA2: F'frd 6G **23**
Crown Ct. BA15: Brad A 4H **25**
Crown Hill BA1: W'ton 6D **10**
Crown Rd. BA1: W'ton 6C **10**
Croxham Orchard BA1: Bathe 3E **13**
Cuckoo La. BS39: Clut, High L 5D **36**
Cuckoo Wlk. BA14: Trow 1F **33**
Culverhay Sports Cen. 1C 20
Culver Rd. BA15: Brad A 6H **25**
Culvers Cl. BS31: Key 1D **6**
Culvers Rd. BS31: Key 1D **6**
Cumberland Ho. BA1: Bath 4B **4**
Cumberland Row BA1: Bath 4C **4** (3G **17**)
Cusance Way BA14: Hilp 4G **31**
Cygnet Way BA14: Stav 6E **27**
Cynthia Rd. BA2: Bath 4D **16**
Cynthia Vs. BA2: Bath 4D **16**
Cypress Ter. BA3: Rads 4H **45**

D

Dafford's Bldgs. BA1: Bath 5B **12**
Dafford's Pl. *BA1: Bath 5B 12*
(off Dafford St.)
Dafford St. BA1: Bath 5B **12**
Daglands, The BA2: Cam 3D **40**
Dahlia Gdns. BA2: Bath 2H **5** (2A **18**)
Dairy Hill BA2: Ston L 6F **43**
Daisey Bank BA2: Bath 5A **18**
Damson Orchard BA1: Bathe 3F **13**
Daneacre Rd. BA3: Rads 2C **46**
Dane Cl. BA15: W'ley 4B **24**
Dane Ri. BA15: W'ley 4B **24**
Daniel M. BA2: Bath 2G **5** (2A **18**)
Daniel St. BA2: Bath 2G **5** (2A **18**)
Dapp's Hill BS31: Key 2E **7**
Dark La. BA2: Batham 6E **13**
BA2: F'frd 6G **23**
BS40: Chew M 2D **34**
Darlington M. BA2: Bath 3G **5** (2A **18**)
Darlington Pl. BA2: Bath 5H **5** (3A **18**)
Darlington Rd. BA2: Bath 2H **5** (2A **18**)
Darlington St. BA2: Bath 3G **5** (2A **18**)
Darlington Wharf BA2: Bath 1H **5** (1A **18**)
Dartmouth Av. BA2: Bath 4D **16**
Dartmouth Wlk. BS31: Key 3C **6**
Day Cres. BA2: Bath 3A **16**
Deadmill La. BA1: Swa 4B **12**
Deanery Wlk. BA2: Lim S 5H **23**
DEAN HILL 5A 10
Deanhill La. BA1: W'ton 5A **10**
Delamere Rd. BA14: Trow 3E **31**
De Montalt Pl. BA2: C Down 2A **22**
Dene Cl. BS31: Key 4E **7**
Denmark Rd. BA2: Bath 3E **17**
Denny La. BS40: Chew M 5E **35**
Derwent Gro. BS31: Key 2F **7**
Deverell Cl. BA15: Brad A 1H **29**
Deveron Gro. BS31: Key 3F **7**
Devizes Rd. BA14: Hilp 2H **31**
Devonshire Bldgs. BA2: Bath 5G **17**
(not continuous)
Devonshire M. *BA1: Bath 3H 17*
(off St James's Pde.)
BA2: Bath 6G 17
(off Devonshire Bldgs.)
Devonshire Pl. BA2: Bath 5G **17**
Devonshire Rd. BA2: Batham 6D **12**
Devonshire Vs. BA2: Bath 6G **17**
Dixon Gdns. BA1: Bath 6G **11**
Dominion Rd. BA2: Bath 3B **16**
Donnington Wlk. BS31: Key 3C **6**
Dorchester St. BA1: Bath 6E **5** (4H **17**)
Doric Bus. Cen. BA14: Trow 2E **31**
DOROTHY HOUSE HOSPICE CARE 5A 24
Dorset Cl. BA2: Bath 3E **17**
Dorset Cotts. BA2: C Down 2B **22**
Dorset Ho. BA2: Bath 6E **17**
Dorset St. BA2: Bath 3E **17**
DOUBLE HILL 4D 42
Dovecote Cl. BA14: Trow 5C **30**
Dover Ho. BA1: Bath 1H **17**
Dover Pl. BA1: Bath 1H **17**
Dovers La. BA1: Bathf 5H **13**

Dovers Pk. BA1: Bathf 5H **13**
Dover Ter. *BA1: Bath* *1A* ***18***
(off London Rd.)
Dowding Rd. BA1: Bath 6A **12**
Dowding Vs. BA1: Bath 6A **12**
Down, The BA14: Trow 3E **31**
Down Av. BA2: C Down 2H **21**
Downavon BA15: Brad A 6G **25**
Downfield BS31: Key 2C **6**
Downhayes Rd. BA14: Trow 3E **31**
Down La. BA2: Batham 6E **13**
Downs, The BA3: Clan 6E **41**
Downs Cl. BA15: Brad A 4E **25**
Downside Cl. BA2: Batham 6E **13**
Downside Pk. BA14: Trow 3F **31**
Downside Vw. BA14: Trow 3F **31**
Downs Vw. BA15: Brad A 4E **25**
Downsway BS39: Paul 5F **39**
Down Vw. BA3: Hay 5B **46**
Dragons Hill Cl. BS31: Key 2E **7**
Dragons Hill Ct. BS31: Key 2E **7**
Dragons Hill Gdns. BS31: Key 2E **7**
Drake Av. BA2: C Down 1G **21**
Drake Cl. BS31: Salt 5A **8**
Dransfield Way BA2: Bath 5D **16**
Draycott Ct. BA2: Bath 2F **5** (2H **17**)
Dring, The BA3: Rads 3A **46**
Drinkwater Ct. BA14: Trow 6E **31**
Drive, The BS31: Key 1D **6**
Drungway BA2: Mon C 2D **22**
Dryleaze BS31: Key 1D **6**
DRYNHAM **2F 33**
Drynham Drove BA14: Trow 3E **33**
Drynham La. BA14: Trow 1E **33**
Drynham Pk. BA14: Trow 1E **33**
Drynham Rd. BA14: Trow 1E **33**
Duchy Cl. BA3: Clan 6E **41**
Duchy Rd. BA3: Clan 6E **41**
Dudley Cl. BS31: Key 3D **6**
Duke St. BA2: Bath 5F **5** (3H **17**)
BA14: Trow 4E **31**
Dumpers La. BS40: Chew M 3E **35**
Duncan Gdns. BA1: W'ton 4B **10**
Dundas Aqueduct **1F 23**
Dunford Cl. BA14: Trow 1E **33**
Dunkerton Hill BA2: Dunk, Pea J 2B **42**
Dunsford Pl. BA2: Bath 4H **5** (3A **18**)
Dunster Ho. BA2: C Down 1H **21**
Dunster Rd. BS31: Key 3C **6**
Durcott La. BA2: Cam, Tim 3C **40**
Durham Gro. BS31: Key 3C **6**
Durley Hill BS31: Key 1C **6**
Durley Pk. BA2: Bath 5F **17**
DURSLEY **6F 33**
Dursley Rd. BA14: Hey 6F **33**
BA14: Trow 6D **30**
Dymboro, The BA3: Mid N 4D **44**
Dymboro Av. BA3: Mid N 4D **44**
Dymboro Cl. BA3: Mid N 4D **44**
Dymboro Gdns. BA3: Mid N 4D **44**
Dymott Sq. BA14: Hilp 2H **31**

E

Eagle Cotts. BA1: Bathe 2E **13**
Eagle Pk. BA1: Bathe 2E **13**
BA14: Trow .1F **33**
Eagle Rd. BA1: Bathe 2E **13**
Eastbourne Av. BA1: Bath 6A **12**
Eastbourne Gdns. BA14: Trow 4F **31**
Eastbourne Rd. BA14: Trow 4F **31**
Eastbourne Vs. BA1: Bath 6A **12**
East Cl. BA2: Bath 4B **16**
Eastcourt Rd. BS39: Temp C 3A **38**
Eastdown Pl. *BA3: Clan* *6E* ***41***
(off Eastdown Rd.)
Eastdown Rd. BA3: Clan 6E **41**
Eastfield Av. BA1: W'ton 4C **10**
East La. BA14: B Gif, Holt 1H **27**
East La. Bus. Pk. BA14: Holt 1H **27**
E. Lea Rd. BA1: Bath 1B **16**
Eastmead BA3: Mid N 3F **45**
Easton Ho. BA1: Bath 6B **12**
Eastover Gro. BA2: Odd D 2D **20**
Eastover Rd. BS39: High L 2F **39**
EAST TWERTON **3E 17**
Eastview Rd. BA14: Trow 6B **30**
Eastville BA1: Bath 6A **12**
East Way BA2: Bath 4B **16**
Eastwood BA2: Batham 3D **18**
Eastwood Cl. BS39: High L 1F **39**
Eastwoods BA1: Bathf 4G **13**
Ebenezer Ter. BA2: Bath 6F **5**
Eckweek Gdns. BA2: Pea J 3B **42**
Eckweek La. BA2: Pea J 3B **42**
Eckweek Rd. BA2: Pea J 3B **42**
Eden Pk. Cl BA1: Bathe 3F **13**
Eden Pk. Dr. BA1: Bathe 3F **13**
Eden Ter. BA1: Bath 5A **12**
Eden Vs. *BA1: Bath* *5B* ***12***
(off Dafford's Bldgs.)
Edgar Bldgs. BA1: Bath 3D **4**
Edgeworth Rd. BA2: Bath 6D **16**
Edinburgh Rd. BS31: Key 3D **6**
Edward St. BA1: Bath 2D **16**
BA2: Bath 3G **5** (2A **18**)
Egerton Rd. BA2: Bath 5F **17**
Egg Theatre, The **4D 4**
Elcombe Cl. BA14: Trow 2D **32**
Eldon Pl. BA1: Bath 5A **12**
Eleanor Cl. BA2: Bath 4A **16**
Ellen Ho. BA2: Bath 4B **16**
Elliot Pl. BA14: Trow 4B **30**
Elliston Dr. BA2: Bath 5C **16**
Ellsbridge Cl. BS31: Key 2G **7**
Elm Cl. BA14: N Bra 4D **32**
BA14: Stav .5E **27**
Elm Ct. BS31: Key 3B **6**
Elmcroft BA1: Bath 5B **12**
Elm Cross Bus. Pk. BA15: Brad A 1F **29**
Elm Cross Shop. Cen. BA15: Brad A 1F **29**
Elmdale Ct. BA14: Trow 6B **30**
Elmdale Rd. BA14: Trow 6B **30**
Elmfield BA15: Brad A 4F **25**
Elm Gro. BA1: Swa 5B **12**
BA2: Bath 5D **16**
Elm Hayes Vw. BS39: Paul 6G **39**
Elmhurst Est. BA1: Bathe 3F **13**
Elm Pl. BA2: Bath 5G **17**
Elm Rd. BS39: Paul 6G **39**
Elms, The BA1: Bath 5B **12**
BA2: Tim 1B **40**
BA14: Holt 2F **27**
(not continuous)
BA15: Brad A 3E **25**
Elms Cross BA15: Brad A 2E **29**
Elms Cross Dr. BA15: Brad A 6F **25**
Elms Cross Vineyard **2F 29**
Elm Ter. BA3: Rads 4G **45**
Elm Tree Av. BA3: Rads 4H **45**
Elm Vw. BA3: Mid N 3F **45**
Empress Menen Gdns. BA1: Bath 1B **16**
Enfield Cl. BA15: West 2C **28**
Enginehouse La. BS31: Q Char 3A **6**
ENGLISHCOMBE **1A 20**
Englishcombe La. BA2: Bath 6C **16**
Englishcombe Ri. BA2: Bath 6B **16**
Englishcombe Rd. BA2: Eng 1A **20**
Englishcombe Way BA2: Bath 6F **17**
Entry Hill BA2: Bath, C Down 6G **17**
Entry Hill Dr. BA2: Bath 6G **17**
Entry Hill Gdns. BA2: Bath 6G **17**
Entry Hill Pk. BA2: C Down 1G **21**
Entry Ri. BA2: C Down 2G **21**
Epsom Rd. BA14: Trow 3F **33**
Epsom Sq. BA14: Trow 3F **33**
Ethendune Ct. BA14: Trow 4F **31**
Eveleigh Av. BA1: Swa 5C **12**
Eveleigh Ho. *BA2: Bath* *3E* ***5***
(off Grove St.)
Evelyn Rd. BA1: Bath 1C **16**
Evelyn Ter. BA1: Bath 6H **11**
Evenlode Way BS31: Key 4F **7**
Everleigh Cl. BA14: Trow 2E **33**
Excelsior St. BA2: Bath 6F **5** (4A **18**)
Excelsior Ter. BA3: Mid N 4F **45**
Excel Tennis Cen. . . . .**3C 4 (2G 17)**
Exmoor Rd. BA2: C Down 1G **21**

F

Fairacres Cl. BS31: Key 2D **6**
Fairfield Av. BA1: Bath 5H **11**
Fairfield Mdws. BA14: S'wick 4A **32**
FAIRFIELD PARK **5H 11**
Fairfield Pk. Rd. BA1: Bath 5G **11**
Fairfield Rd. BA1: Bath 6H **11**
Fairfield Ter. BA1: Bath 5H **11**
BA2: Pea J 4A **42**
Fairfield Vw. BA1: Bath 5H **11**
Fairhaven Cotts. BA1: Bathe 1F **13**
Fairseat Ind. Est. BS40: Chew S 6C **34**
Fairways BS31: Salt 5B **8**
Fairwood Cl. BA14: Hilp 3H **31**
Falcon Dr. BA14: Trow 6F **31**
Falconer Rd. BA1: W'ton 4B **10**
Farleigh Av. BA14: Trow 6B **30**
FARLEIGH HUNGERFORD **5B 28**
Farleigh Hungerford Castle **5B 28**
Farleigh Ri. BA1: Bathf 5H **13**
Farleigh Rd. BA14: Wing 5D **28**
BS31: Key 3C **6**
Farleigh Vw. *BA1: Bath* *6H* ***11***
(off Richmond La.)
BA15: West .2C **28**
FARMBOROUGH **3H 37**
Farm Cl. BA14: Trow 4C **30**
Farm La. BA2: Wel 2H **43**
Farrington Flds. BS39: Far G 2A **44**
Farrington Flds. Trad. Est.
BS39: Far G .2A **44**
Farrington Rd. BS39: Far G, Paul 6E **39**
Farr's La. BA2: C Down 1A **22**
Faulkland La. BA2: Ston L 6G **43**
BA3: Faul, Fox 6G **43**
Faulkland Rd. BA2: Bath 4E **17**
Faulkland Vw. BA2: Pea J 4C **42**
Faverolle Way BA14: Hilp 3H **31**
Featherbed La. BS39: Clut, Stan W 5A **36**
Fenton Cl. BS31: Salt 4A **8**
Fern Cl. BA3: Mid N 5F **45**
Ferndale Rd. BA1: Swa 4B **12**
Ferris Way BA14: Hilp 4G **31**
Ferry La. BA2: Bath 5F **5** (3A **18**)
BA2: C'ton .4H **19**
Fersfield BA2: Bath 6A **18**
Fieldgardens Rd. BS39: Temp C 2B **38**
Fieldings Rd. BA2: Bath 3D **16**
Fieldins BA15: W'ley 4B **24**
Filer Cl. BA2: Pea J 3B **42**
Firgrove La. BA2: Pea J 2H **41**
Firs, The BA2: C Down 2A **22**
BA2: Lim S .6F **23**
Firs Ct. BS31: Key 3B **6**
Firs Hill BA14: S'wick 3B **32**
First Av. BA2: Bath 5E **17**
BA3: Mid N .5G **45**
Fir Tree Av. BS39: Paul 1D **44**
Fitness First Health Club
Bath ***5C 4***
(off James St. W.)
Fitzmaurice Cl. BA15: Brad A 1H **29**
Fitzmaurice Pl. BA15: Brad A 6G **25**
Fitzroy Ho. BA2: Bath 3F **5** (2H **17**)
Five Arches Cl. BA3: Mid N 3H **45**
Flat, The BS39: Clut 4A **36**
Flatwoods Cres. BA2: C'ton D 6E **19**
Flatwoods Rd. BA2: C'ton D 6E **19**
Fleece Cotts. BA14: Trow 6F **31**
Fleur-de-Lys Dr. BA14: S'wick 3A **32**
Florida Ter. BA3: Mid N 3G **45**
Folly, The BS31: Salt 5C **8**
Folly Cl. BA3: Mid N 6C **44**
Folly Fld. BA15: Brad A 1G **29**

Fonthill Rd. BA1: L'dwn 5F **11**
Ford Rd. BA2: Pea J 3A **42**
Forefield Pl. BA2: Bath 4H **17**
Forefield Ri. BA2: Bath 5H **17**
Forefield Ter. BA2: Bath 4A **18**
Forester Av. BA2: Bath 1F **5** (1H **17**)
Forester Ct. BA2: Bath 1F **5** (1H **17**)
Forester La. BA2: Bath 1G **5** (1A **18**)
Forester Rd. BA2: Bath 2G **5** (2A **18**)
Fore St. BA14: Trow 4E **31**
FOREWOODS COMMON **4C 26**
Fortescue Rd. BA3: Rads 3B **46**
Forum Bldgs. *BA1: Bath 6E **5***
(off St James's Pde.)
Fosse Cott. BA3: Mid N 2H **45**
Fossefield Rd. BA3: Mid N 6F **45**
Fosse Gdns. BA2: Odd D 3E **21**
Fosse Grn. BA3: Clan 1A **46**
Fosse La. BA1: Bathe 4F **13**
BA3: Mid N 2G **45**
Fosseway BA2: Dunk 5A **20**
BA3: Mid N 6G **45**
Fosse Way Cl. BA2: Pea J 4A **42**
Fosse Way Est. BA2: Odd D 2D **20**
Fosseway Gdns. BA3: Rads 4H **45**
Fosseway Sth. BA3: Mid N 6F **45**
Foss Way BA2: Pea J 5H **41**
BA3: Mid N, Rads 6F **41**
BA3: Rads 4H **45**
Fossway BA3: Clan 1A **46**
Foundry Wlk. *BS39: Paul 5F **39***
(off Church St.)
Fountain Bldgs. BA1: Bath 3E **5** (2H **17**)
Fourth Av. BA3: Mid N 5H **45**
Fox & Hounds La. BS31: Key 2E **7**
Foxcombe Rd. BA1: Bath 2C **16**
FOXCOTE **1H 47**
Foxcote Av. BA2: Pea J 4B **42**
Foxglove Dr. BA14: Trow 1F **31**
FOX HILL **1A 22**
Fox Hill BA2: C Down 2H **21**
Foxhill Ho. BA2: C Down 2H **21**
FOX HILLS **4C 46**
Frampton Ct. BA14: Trow 1B **32**
Francis St. BA14: Trow 4D **30**
Frankcom Ho. BA2: Bath 1G **5** (2A **18**)
Frankland Cl. BA1: Bath 6B **10**
Frankley Bldgs. BA1: Bath 6A **12**
Frankley Ter. *BA1: Bath 6A **12***
(off Snow Hill)
Frederick Av. BA2: Pea J 4A **42**
Freeview Rd. BA2: Bath 3B **16**
French Cl. BA2: Pea J 4B **42**
Frenchfield Rd. BA2: Pea J 4B **42**
FRESHFORD **6G 23**
Freshford La. BA2: F'frd 6F **23**
Freshford Station (Rail) **6H 23**
Friary Cl. BA15: West 1B **28**
Frome Old Rd. BA3: Rads 3C **46**
Frome Rd. BA2: Odd D 1D **20**
BA3: Rads, Writ 3B **46**
BA14: S'wick, Trow 4A **32**
(not continuous)
BA14: Wing 6F **29**
BA15: Brad A 2F **29**
FRYS BOTTOM **4C 36**
Frys Leaze BA1: Bath 5A **12**
Fulford Rd. BA14: Trow 3F **31**
Fuller Rd. BA1: Bath 5B **12**
Fullers Way BA2: Odd D 3E **21**
Fulney Cl. BA14: Trow 3G **31**
Furlong Cl. BA3: Mid N 6D **44**
Furlong Gdns. BA14: Trow 4F **31**
Furnleaze BS39: Clut 6A **36**

G

Gainsborough Gdns. BA1: Bath 1D **16**
Gainsborough Ri. BA14: Trow 1B **32**
Gainsborough Rd. BS31: Key 2E **7**
Garfield Ter. BA1: Bath 5B **12**
Garre Ho. BA2: Bath 4A **16**
Garrick Rd. BA2: Bath 4A **16**
Garstons BA1: Bathf 5H **13**
Garth Rd. BA14: Hilp 4G **31**
Gaston BA14: Holt 3F **27**
Gaston Av. BS31: Key 1E **7**
Gateway, The BA14: Trow 5D **30**
Gay Ct. BA1: Bathe 4D **12**
Gay's Hill BA1: Bath 1H **17**
Gay St. BA1: Bath 3D **4** (2G **17**)
Geldof Dr. BA3: Mid N 3E **45**
George's Bldgs. BA1: Bath 1E **5** (1H **17**)
George's Pl. BA2: Bath 4H **5**
George's Rd. BA1: Bath 6H **11**
George St. BA1: Bath 3D **4** (2G **17**)
BA2: Bath 4H **5** (3A **18**)
BA14: Trow 4E **31**
Georgian Garden **3C 4 (2G 17)**
Georgian Ho. BA2: Bath 5F **5**
Georgian Vw. BA2: Bath 6D **16**
Gerrard Bldgs. BA2: Bath 3G **5** (2H **17**)
Gibbs Leaze BA14: Hilp 4H **31**
Giffords, The BA14: Hilp 1H **31**
Gillet's Hill La. BS39: Temp C 3A **38**
Gillingham Ter. BA1: Bath 6A **12**
Gipsy La. BA14: Holt 1G **27**
Gladstone Pl. BA2: C Down 2B **22**
Gladstone Rd. BA2: C Down 1B **22**
BA14: Trow 6C **30**
Gladstone St. BA3: Mid N 2F **45**
Glebe, The BA2: F'frd 6G **23**
BA2: Tim 1B **40**
Glebe Ho. *BA2: Bath 6G **5***
(off Widcombe Hill)
Glebelands BA3: Rads 4H **45**
Glebe Rd. BA2: Bath 5C **16**
BA14: Trow 6B **30**
Glebe Wlk. BS31: Key 3B **6**
Glen, The BS31: Salt 6C **8**
Glencairn Ct. BA2: Bath 4G **5** (3A **18**)
Gloster Vs. BA1: Bath 1E **5** (1H **17**)
Gloucester Rd. BA1: Bath, Swa 2B **12**
BA1: Up Swa 1A **12**
BA14: Trow 6C **30**
Gloucester St. BA1: Bath 2C **4** (2G **17**)
Goldney Cl. BS39: Temp C 2A **38**
Goldney Way BS39: Temp C 2A **38**
Golf Club La. BS31: Salt 5B **8**
Golf Course Rd. BA2: Bath 3B **18**
Goodwood Cl. BA14: Trow 3F **33**
Goold Cl. BA2: Cor 1D **14**
Goosard La. BS39: High L 3F **39**
Gooseberry La. BS31: Key 2E **7**
Goose St. BA14: S'wick 5B **32**
Gordon Bldgs. *BA3: Rads 2C **46***
(off Woodborough Rd.)
Gordon Rd. BA2: Bath 4A **18**
BA2: Pea J 3B **42**
Gores Pk. BS39: High L 1D **38**
Governors Ho. BA2: Bath 3E **17**
Grace Dr. BA3: Mid N 3E **45**
Grand Pde. BA2: Bath 4E **5** (3H **17**)
Grange End BA3: Mid N 6F **45**
Grange Rd. BS31: Salt 5H **7**
Grange Vw. BA15: Brad A 4H **25**
Granville Rd. BA1: L'dwn 4F **11**
Grasmere BA14: Trow 3F **31**
Gravel, The BA14: Holt 2F **27**
Gravel Hill BS40: Up Str, Chew S 6A **34**
Gravel Wlk. BA1: Bath 2B **4** (2F **17**)
Grays Hill BA2: Ston L 5F **43**
Grays Leaze BA14: N Bra 5D **32**
GREAT ASHLEY **2D 24**
Gt. Bedford St. BA1: Bath 1C **4**
Great Parks BA14: Holt 2G **27**
Gt. Pulteney St. BA2: Bath 3F **5** (2H **17**)
Gt. Stanhope St. BA1: Bath 4B **4** (3F **17**)
Green, The BA2: Odd D 2E **21**
Greenacres BA1: W'ton 4C **10**
BA3: Mid N 4C **44**
Greenbank Gdns. BA1: W'ton 6C **10**
Greenbank Vw. BA14: Trow 1A **32**
Green Cl. BA14: Holt 3G **27**
BS39: Paul 5G **39**
Green Cotts. BA2: C Down 2B **22**
Green Ditch La. BA3: Clapt 6A **44**
Greendown Pl. BA2: C Down 2H **21**
Greenfield Wlk. BA3: Mid N 2E **45**
Greenhill Gdns. BA14: Hilp 1H **31**
Greenhill Pl. BA3: Mid N 2E **45**
Greenhill Rd. BA3: Mid N 2E **45**
Greenland Mills BA15: Brad A 5H **25**
Greenlands Rd. BA2: Pea J 3A **42**
Greenland Vw. BA15: Brad A 5H **25**
Green La. BA14: Trow 5F **31**
BA15: Tur 5C **24**
BS39: Far G, Hall 6A **38**
(not continuous)
Green Pk. BA1: Bath 5B **4**
Green Pk. Ho. BA1: Bath 5C **4**
Green Pk. M. BA1: Bath 5B **4** (3F **17**)
Green Pk. Rd. BA1: Bath 5C **4** (3G **17**)
Green Pk. Sta. BA1: Bath 4C **4** (3F **17**)
GREEN PARLOUR **4F 47**
Green Parlour Rd. BA3: Writ 4F **47**
Greenridge BS39: Clut 6B **36**
GREENSBROOK **6B 36**
Green St. BA1: Bath 4D **4** (3G **17**)
BA2: Shos 6B **42**
Green Ter. BA14: Trow 3D **30**
Green Tree Rd. BA3: Mid N 2F **45**
GREENVALE **2B 40**
Greenvale Cl. BA2: Tim 2B **40**
Greenvale Dr. BA2: Tim 2B **40**
Greenvale Rd. BS39: Paul 6F **39**
Greenway Ct. BA2: Bath 5G **17**
Greenway Gdns. BA14: Trow 2F **31**
Greenway La. BA2: Bath 6G **17**
Gregorys Gro. BA2: Odd D 3E **21**
Gregory's Tyning BS39: Paul 5G **39**
GREYFIELD **1E 39**
Greyfield Comn. BS39: High L 1E **39**
Greyfield Rd. BS39: High L 1E **39**
Greyfield Vw. BS39: Temp C 2B **38**
Griffin Ct. BA1: Bath 5C **4**
Grosvenor Bri. Rd. BA1: Bath 6B **12**
Grosvenor Pk. BA1: Bath 6B **12**
Grosvenor Pl. BA1: Bath 6B **12**
Grosvenor Ter. BA1: Bath 5B **12**
Grosvenor Vs. BA1: Bath 6A **12**
Ground Cnr. BA14: Holt 3E **27**
Grove, The BA1: W'ton 6D **10**
BS39: Hall 4D **38**
Grove Ct. BA14: Trow 1D **32**
Grove Ho. BA2: Bath 4G **5**
Grove Leaze BA15: Brad A 5E **25**
Grove St. BA2: Bath 3E **5** (2H **17**)
Grove Wood Rd. BA3: Hay 5A **46**
Gug, The BS39: High L 1E **39**
Guildhall Market 4E 5
(off High St.)
Guinea La. BA1: Bath 2D **4** (2G **17**)
Gullen BA2: Shos, Ston L 6D **42**
Gullock Tyning BA3: Mid N 4F **45**
Gypsy La. BS31: Key 1A **14**

H

Hackett Pl. BA14: Hilp 4H **31**
Haden Rd. BA14: Trow 6E **31**
Hadley Rd. BA2: C Down 1A **22**
Ha Ha, The BA2: Tim 1A **40**
Halfway Cl. BA14: Trow 3G **31**
HALLATROW **4D 38**
Hallatrow Bus. Pk. BS39: Hall 5C **38**
Hallatrow Rd. BS39: Hall, Paul 4D **38**
Halve, The BA14: Trow 4E **31**
HAM **6H 39**
Ham Cl. BA14: Holt 3E **27**
BS39: Temp C 2B **38**
Ham Gdns. BA1: Bath 5E **5** (3H **17**)
BA3: Mid N 4F **45**
HAM GREEN **3E 27**

Ham Gro. BS39: Paul 6G 39
Ham Hill BA3: Rads 2B 46
Hamilton Ho. BA1: L'dwn 4E 11
Hamilton Rd. BA1: Bath 5F 11
Hamilton Ter. BA2: Shos 6D 42
Ham La. BS39: Far G 6A 38
BS39: Paul 6G 39
Hamlet's Yd. BS31: Key 2D 6
Hammond Way BA14: Trow 1E 31
Hampton Ho. BA1: Bath 6B 12
Hampton Row BA2: Bath 1H 5 (1A 18)
Hampton Vw. BA1: Bath 6A 12
Ham Ter. BA14: Holt 3E 27
Handel Rd. BS31: Key 2C 6
Hanewell Ri. BA14: Hilp 5H 31
Hang Hill BA2: Shos, Ston L 5C 42
Hanham La. BS39: Paul 4H 39
Hanna Cl. BA2: Bath 3B 16
Hanny's La. BS40: Chew M 2G 35
Hanover Cl. BA14: Trow 1F 31
Hanover Ct. BA1: Bath 6A 12
BA3: Writ 3D 46
Hanover Pl. BA1: Bath 1A 18
(off London Rd.)
Hanover St. BA1: Bath 6A 12
Hanover Ter. BA1: Bath 6A 12
(off Gillingham Ter.)
Hansford Cl. BA2: C Down 2F 21
Hansford M. BA2: C Down 2G 21
Hansford Sq. BA2: C Down 2F 21
Hantone Hill BA2: Batham 1E 19
Harbutts BA2: Batham 6E 13
Harcourt Cl. BS31: Salt 5B 8
Harcourt Gdns. BA1: W'ton 5C 10
Harding Pl. BS31: Key 2G 7
Hardington Dr. BS31: Key 5F 7
Hare Knapp BA15: Brad A 5E 25
Harford Sq. BS40: Chew M 2F 35
Harford St. BA14: Trow 4F 31
Hargreaves Rd. BA14: Trow 6F 31
Harington Ct. BA2: New L 4E 15
Harington Pl. BA1: Bath 4D 4 (3G 17)
Harlech Cl. BS31: Key 3B 6
Harley St. BA1: Bath 1C 4 (1G 17)
Harmony Pl. BA14: Trow 6E 31
HARTLEY 3B 24
Hart's La. BS39: Hall 4C 38
Harts Paddock BA3: Mid N 2D 44
Haselbury Gro. BS31: Salt 5B 8
Hassage Hill BA2: Wel 3H 43
Hatfield Bldgs. BA2: Bath 6G 5 (4A 18)
Hatfield Rd. BA2: Bath 6F 17
Havelock Ct. BA14: Trow 6D 30
(off Havelock St.)
Havelock St. BA14: Trow 6D 30
Haviland Gro. BA1: W'ton 4B 10
Haviland Pk. BA1: W'ton 5C 10
Havory BA1: Bath 6B 12
Hawarden Ter. BA1: Bath 6A 12
Hawcroft BA14: Holt 2F 27
Hawkeridge Rd. BA14: Hey, Yarn 6F 33
BA14: N Bra 5G 33
Hawthorn Ct. BS31: Key 2D 6
Hawthorn Gro. BA2: C Down 2G 21
BA14: Trow 2D 32
Hawthorn Rd. BA3: Rads 3D 46
Hawthorns La. BS31: Key 2D 6
Hayboro Way BS39: Paul 1C 44
Haycombe Crematorium BA2: Bath 5A 16
Haycombe Dr. BA2: Bath 4B 16
Haycombe La. BA2: Eng 6A 16
Hayden Cl. BA2: Bath 4F 17
HAYDON 5B 46
Haydon Ga. BA3: Hay 5B 46
Haydon Hill BA3: Hay 5B 46
Haydon Ind. Est. BA3: Hay 5B 46
Hayes Cl. BA14: Trow 2F 31
Hayesfield Pk. BA2: Bath 4G 17
HAYES PARK 3D 44
Hayes Pk. Rd. BA3: Mid N 3D 44
Hayes Pl. BA2: Bath 5G 17
Hayes Rd. BA3: Mid N 3D 44
Hayeswood Rd. BA2: Tim 5F 37
Haygarth Ct. BA1: Bath 1D 4 (1G 17)
Hay Hill BA1: Bath 2D 4 (2G 17)
Hazel Gro. BA2: Bath 5E 17
BA3: Mid N 5F 45
BA14: Trow 2C 32
Hazel Ter. BA3: Mid N 5F 45
Hazel Way BA2: Odd D 3E 21
Hazleton Gdns. BA2: C'ton D 6E 19
Heather Dr. BA2: Odd D 3E 21
Heather Shaw BA14: Trow 5F 31
Heathfield Cl. BA1: W'ton 4B 10
BS31: Key 2B 6
Hebden Rd. BA15: West 2C 28
Heddington Cl. BA14: Trow 2D 32
Hedgemead Ct. BA1: Bath 1E 5
Helens Ct. BA14: Trow 4D 30
Helmdon Rd. BA14: Trow 4B 30
Helps Well Rd. BA14: Hilp 6H 31
Henderson Cl. BA14: Trow 6C 30
Henley Vw. BA2: Wel 2H 43
Henrietta Ct. BA2: Bath 1F 5 (1H 17)
Henrietta Gdns. BA2: Bath 2F 5 (2H 17)
Henrietta M. BA2: Bath 3F 5 (2H 17)
Henrietta Pl. BA2: Bath 3E 5 (2H 17)
Henrietta Rd. BA2: Bath 2F 5 (2H 17)
Henrietta St. BA2: Bath 3F 5 (2H 17)
Henrietta Vs. BA2: Bath 2F 5 (2H 17)
Henry St. BA1: Bath 5E 5 (3H 17)
Hensley Gdns. BA2: Bath 5F 17
Hensley Rd. BA2: Bath 5F 17
Herbert Rd. BA2: Bath 4E 17
Herbleaze BA14: Stav 6E 27
Heritage, The BA2: Cam 3E 41
Heritage Cl. BA2: Pea J 3B 42
Hermes Cl. BS31: Salt 5A 8
Hermitage Rd. BA1: Bath 6F 11
Heron Wlk. BA14: Trow 1F 33
Herschel Mus. of Astronomy, The
. . . . .4C 4 (3G 17)
Herschel Pl. BA2: Bath 2G 5 (2H 17)
Hetling Ct. BA1: Bath 5D 4 (3G 17)
Hewitt Cl. BA14: Trow 6F 31
Hexagon, The BA2: Odd D 2F 21
High Acre BS39: Paul 1D 44
High Bannerdown BA1: Bathe 3G 13
Highbury Farm Bus. Pk. BS39: Hall 3C 38
Highbury Pl. BA1: Bath 6H 11
Highbury Rd. BS39: Hall 3D 38
Highbury Ter. BA1: Bath 6H 11
Highbury Vs. BA1: Bath 6H 11
(off Highbury Pl.)
High Energy Fitness Studio 4F 45
Highfield Cl. BA2: Bath 4C 16
Highfield Rd. BA2: Pea J 3A 42
BA15: Brad A 4G 25
BS31: Key 5E 7
Highfields BA3: Rads 3H 45
Highland Rd. BA2: Bath 4C 16
Highland Ter. BA2: Bath 3E 17
HIGH LITTLETON 2F 39
High Mdws. BA3: Mid N 4D 44
High Pk. BS39: Paul 5F 39
High St. BA1: Bath 4E 5 (3H 17)
BA1: Bathe 4E 13
BA1: Bathf 5H 13
BA1: W'ly .1G 11
BA1: W'ton 5C 10
BA2: Bath .3B 16
BA2: Batham 6E 13
BA2: F'frd .6G 23
BA2: Tim 1B 40
BA2: Wel 2H 43
BA3: Mid N 4E 45
BS31: Key 1D 6
BS31: Salt 4B 8
BS39: High L 2E 39
BS39: Paul .5G 39
(not continuous)
BS40: Chew M 2E 35
High Vw. BA2: Bath 6B 4 (4F 17)
Hilbury Ct. BA14: Trow 4F 31
Hill, The BA2: F'frd 6H 23
Hill Av. BA2: C Down 2G 21
Hill Ct. BS39: Paul 5G 39
Hillcrest BA2: Pea J 3A 42
Hillcrest Dr. BA2: Bath 5C 16
Hillcrest Flats BA15: Brad A 4H 25
Hills Cl. BS31: Key 2F 7
HILLSIDE 5C 44
Hillside Av. BA3: Mid N 5C 44
Hillside Cl. BS39: Paul 5H 39
Hillside Cotts. BA2: Mid 5A 22
Hillside Cres. BA3: Mid N 5C 44
Hillside Rd. BA2: Bath 5E 17
BA3: Mid N 5D 44
Hillside Vw. BA2: Pea J 3A 42
BA3: Mid N 3E 45
Hill St. BA14: Hilp 1G 31
BA14: Trow 4D 30
Hill St. Ct. BA14: Trow 4D 30
Hillview BA2: Tim 2B 40
BA3: Mid N 6C 44
Hill Vw. Rd. BA1: Bath 5A 12
HILPERTON 2H 31
Hilperton Dr. BA14: Hilp 3H 31
HILPERTON MARSH 1G 31
Hilperton Rd. BA14: Trow 4F 31
Hinton Cl. BA2: Bath 3A 16
BS31: Salt 4B 8
Hiscocks Ct. BA2: New L 3E 15
Hiscocks Dr. BA2: Bath 5F 17
HOBB'S WALL .4G 37
Hobb's Wall BA2: F'boro 4G 37
Hobhouse Cl. BA15: Brad A 1H 29
Hockley Ct. BA1: W'ton 6E 11
Hodshill BA2: S'ske 5G 21
Hoggington La. BA14: S'wick 4A 32
Holbrook La. BA14: Trow 1D 32
Holburne Mus. of Art 2G 5 (2A 18)
Holcombe Cl. BA2: Batham 6E 13
Holcombe Grn. BA1: W'ton 5C 10
(not continuous)
Holcombe Gro. BS31: Key 2C 6
Holcombe La. BA2: Batham 6E 13
Holcombe Va. BA2: Batham 6E 13
Holland Rd. BA1: Bath 6A 12
Hollies, The BA3: Mid N 4E 45
Hollies La. BA1: Bathe 1E 13
Hollis Way BA14: S'wick 4A 32
Hollow, The BA2: Bath 5B 16
Holloway BA2: Bath 6D 4 (4G 17)
Hollowbrook La. BS40: Chew M 6H 35
Hollowpit La. BA3: Hem 6H 47
Hollybush Cl. BA15: W'ley 4B 24
Holly Ct. BA3: Mid N 4F 45
Holly Dr. BA2: Odd D 3E 21
Holly Wlk. BA3: Rads 4A 46
BS31: Key 4C 6
Holmoak Rd. BS31: Key 3B 6
HOLT 2G 27
Holt Rd. BA15: Brad A 5H 25
Holwell Cl. BS39: Paul 1C 44
Holyrood Cl. BA14: Trow 2C 32
Homeavon Ho. BS31: Key 2E 7
Home Cl. BA14: Trow 6E 31
Home Farm Cl. BA2: Pea J 4H 41
Homefield BA2: Tim 1C 40
Homefield Cl. BS31: Salt 4B 8
Homefield Rd. BS31: Salt 4C 8
Homelands BA1: Bathe 3E 13
Homelea Pk. E. BA1: Bath 2B 16
Homelea Pk. W. BA1: Bath 2B 16
Homeleaze BA2: New L 3F 15
Homemead BA2: Cor 1D 14
Home Mill Bldgs. BA14: Trow 5E 31
Home Orchard BS40: Chew S 5B 34
Homestead, The BA14: Trow 6D 30
BS31: Key 5E 7
Honeymans Cl. BA14: Trow 5G 31
Honeysuckle Cl. BA14: Trow 5F 31
Hook BA2: Tim .1D 40
Hook Hill BA2: Tim 1C 40
Hope Nature Cen. 3A 32

Hope Pl. BS39: Paul 6F 39
Hope Ter. BA3: Mid N 4F 45
Hornbeam Rd. BA14: Trow 2D 32
Hornbeam Wlk. BS31: Key 4B 6
Horsecombe Brow BA2: C Down 2H 21
Horsecombe Gro. BA2: C Down 2H 21
Horsecombe Va. BA2: C Down 2H 21
Horse Rd. BA14: Hilp 1F 31
Horseshoe Cl. BA14: Hilp 6H 31
Horseshoe Rd. BA2: Bath 6H 5 (4B 18)
Horseshoe Wlk. BA2: Bath 6H 5 (4A 18)
Horstmann Cl. BA1: Bath 2C 16
Horton Cl. BA15: Brad A 1H 29
Horton Ho. BA2: Bath 1F 5 (1H 17)
Hot Bath St. BA1: Bath 5D 4 (3G 17)
Howard Cl. BS31: Salt 4A 8
How Hill BA2: Bath 3B 16
Huddox Hill BA2: Pea J 3B 42
Huish Cl. BA3: Writ 3E 47
Huish Ct. BA3: Rads 4D 46
Hulbert Cl. BA14: Hilp, Trow 4G 31
Hummingbird Gdns.
    BA14: Trow 1F 33
Hungerford Av. BA14: Trow 6B 30
Hungerford Ct. BA2: New L 4E 15
Hungerford Rd. BA1: Bath 2D 16
Hungerford Ter. BA2: Wel 2H 43
Hunstrete Rd. BA2: F'boro 2H 37
Hunters Rest Miniature Railway 4C 36
Huntingdon Pl. BA15: Brad A 4F 25
Huntingdon Ri. BA15: Brad A 3F 25
Huntingdon St. BA15: Brad A 4F 25
Hurn La. BS31: Key 3E 7
Hutton Cl. BS31: Key 5F 7
Hyde Rd. BA14: Trow 3D 30
Hydes, The BS31: Key 1D 6
Hylton Row BA3: Writ 3E 47

I

Idwal Cl. BA2: Pea J 3A 42
Iford Cl. BS31: Salt 4B 8
Iford Flds. BA15: Ifo 3B 28
Iford Hill BA15: Ifo 3B 28
Iford La. BA2: Ifo 2A 28
    BA15: Ifo .2A 28
Industrial Quarter, The BA2: Pea J . . .4C 42
Inglesham Cl. BA14: Trow 2E 33
Inman Ho. BA1: Bath 6H 11
Inner Elm Ter. BA3: Rads 4G 45
Innox Footpath BA14: Trow 4D 30
Innox Gro. BA2: Eng 1A 20
Innox La. BA1: Up Swa 2A 12
Innox Mill Cl. BA14: Trow 4C 30
Innox Rd. BA2: Swa, Up Swa 2A 12
    BA2: Bath 4C 16
    BA14: Trow 4C 30
Inverness Rd. BA2: Bath 3D 16
Isabella Cotts. BA2: C Down 2A 22
    (off Rock La.)
Isabella M. BA2: C Down 2A 22
Island, The BA3: Mid N 4E 45
Islington BA14: Trow 4E 31
Islington Gdns. BA14: Trow 4E 31
Ivo Peters Rd. BA2: Bath 5B 4 (3F 17)
Ivy Av. BA2: Bath 5D 16
Ivy Bank Pk. BA2: C Down 1G 21
Ivy Cotts. BA2: S'ske 4G 21
Ivy Gro. BA2: Bath 5D 16
Ivy Pl. BA2: Bath 5D 16
Ivy Ter. BA15: Brad A 4G 25
Ivy Vs. BA2: Bath 5D 16
    BA14: Trow 4B 30
Ivy Wlk. BA3: Mid N 5F 45

J

James St. BA14: Trow 3E 31
James St. W. BA1: Bath 4B 4 (3F 17)
Jane Austen Cen. 3D 4

Jasmine Way BA14: Trow 5F 31
    (not continuous)
Jena Ct. BS31: Salt 4A 8
Jenkins St. BA14: Trow 3D 30
Jesse Hughes Ct. BA1: Bath 5B 12
Jew's La. BA2: Bath 3D 16
John Rennie Cl. BA15: Brad A 1H 29
John Slessor Ct. BA1: Bath . . .1D 4 (1G 17)
Johnstone St. BA2: Bath 4F 5 (3H 17)
John St. BA1: Bath 3D 4 (2G 17)
Jones Hill BA15: Brad A 1E 29
Jubilee Rd. BA3: Rads 4H 45
Jubilee Ter. BS39: Paul 5G 39
Julian Cotts. BA2: Mon C 2D 22
Julian Rd. BA1: Bath 1C 4 (1G 17)
Julier Ho. BA1: Bath 1E 5
Junction Av. BA2: Bath 4F 17
Junction Rd. BA2: Bath 6A 4 (4F 17)
    BA15: Brad A 5G 25
Justice Av. BS31: Salt 4B 8

K

Kaynton Mead BA1: Bath 3C 16
Keates Cl. BA14: Trow 4E 31
Keats Rd. BA3: Rads 5F 45
Keel's Hill BA2: Pea J 3A 42
Kelso Pl. BA1: Bath 2E 17
KELSTON 4F 9
Kelston Cl. BS31: Salt 4A 8
Kelston Rd. BA1: Bath 6H 9
    BS31: Key .2C 6
Kelston Vw. BA2: Bath 4A 16
    BS31: Salt .4A 8
Kempthorne La. BA2: Odd D 2F 21
Kenilworth Cl. BS31: Key 3C 6
Kenilworth Ct. BA1: Bath 1A 18
    (off Snow Hill)
Kennet Gdns. BA15: Brad A 6G 25
Kennet Pk. BA2: Batham 6D 12
Kennet Rd. BS31: Key 3F 7
Kennet Way BA14: Trow 2E 31
Kennington Rd. BA1: Bath 2C 16
Kensington Cl. BA14: Trow 3E 31
Kensington Ct. BA1: Bath 6A 12
Kensington Flds. BA14: Trow 6A 30
Kensington Gdns. BA1: Bath 6A 12
Kensington Pl. BA1: Bath 1A 18
Kent La. BA1: Up Swa 1A 12
Kenton Dr. BA14: Trow 4G 31
Kenwood Cl. BA14: Trow 5G 31
Keppel Cl. BS31: Salt 5A 8
Kestrel Av. BA14: Trow 1F 33
Kestrel Pl. BA3: Mid N 5F 45
Kettle La. BA14: W Ash 4H 33
Ketton Cl. BA14: Trow 4B 30
Kew Dr. BA14: Trow 6B 30
Kewstoke Rd. BA2: C Down 1H 21
KEYNSHAM 1D 6
Keynsham By-Pass BS31: Key 1D 6
Keynsham Leisure Cen. 2E 7
Keynsham Rd. BS31: Key 1E 7
Keynsham Station (Rail) 1E 7
Kildare BA2: Bath 3H 5 (2A 18)
Kilkenny La. BA2: Eng, Ing 4A 20
Kilmersdon Rd. BA3: Hay, Kil, Rads . . .5A 46
Kinber Cl. BA1: W'ton 4B 10
King Alfred Way BA15: W'ley 4A 24
King Edward Rd. BA2: Bath 4E 17
Kingfisher Cl. BA14: Trow 1F 33
Kingfisher Ct. BA2: Lim S 5H 23
Kingfisher Dr. BA3: Mid N 5F 45
King Georges Rd. BA2: Bath 4D 16
King La. BS39: Clut 4B 36
Kings Ct. BA1: Bath 4D 4
    (off Parsonage La.)
Kingsdown Rd. BA14: Trow 2D 32
Kingsdown Vw. BA1: Bath 6H 11
Kingsfield BA2: Bath 6D 16
    BA15: Brad A 4G 25
Kingsfield Cl. BA15: Brad A 4G 25

Kingsfield Grange Rd. BA15: Brad A . . .4H 25
Kings Gdns. BA14: Trow 6F 27
Kingsley Pl. BA14: Trow 4B 30
Kingsley Rd. BA3: Rads 4G 45
Kingsmead Ct. BA1: Bath 5C 4
    (off Kingsmead Nth.)
Kingsmead E. BA1: Bath 5C 4 (3G 17)
Kingsmead Ho. BA1: Bath 4C 4
Kingsmead Nth. BA1: Bath 5C 4 (3G 17)
Kingsmead Sq. BA1: Bath 5D 4 (3G 17)
Kingsmead St. BA1: Bath 4D 4 (3G 17)
Kingsmead Ter. BA1: Bath 5D 4
Kingsmead W. BA1: Bath 5C 4 (3G 17)
Kings Oak Mdw. BS39: Clut 1A 38
Kingston Av. BA15: Brad A 6H 25
    BS31: Salt .5H 7
Kingston Bldgs. BA1: Bath 5E 5
    (off York St.)
Kingston Pde. BA1: Bath 5E 5
    (off York St.)
Kingston Rd. BA1: Bath 5E 5 (3H 17)
    BA15: Brad A 5G 25
Kingsway BA2: Bath 6D 16
Kingswood Chase BA14: Trow 1A 32
Kingswood Theatre 5F 11
Kingwell Vw. BS39: High L 1F 39
Kipling Av. BA2: Bath 5G 17
Kipling Rd. BA3: Rads 4G 45
Kitcheners Cl. BA14: Trow 4D 30
Kitley Hill BA3: Mid N 1G 45
Knap, The BA14: Hilp 2H 31
Knightstone Cl. BA2: Pea J 3H 41
Knightstone Ct. BA14: Trow 5E 31
Knightstone Pl. BA1: W'ton 6C 10
Knobsbury Hill BA3: Rads 6F 47
Knobsbury La. BA3: Writ 4E 47
KNOWLE HILL 6G 35
Kyrle Gdns. BA1: Bathe 4E 13
Kyte Way BA14: Trow 1F 33

L

Labbott, The BS31: Key 2D 6
Laburnum Cl. BA3: Mid N 5D 44
Laburnum Gro. BA3: Mid N 5D 44
    BA14: Trow 1C 32
Laburnum Ter. BA1: Bathe 4E 13
Laburnum Wlk. BS31: Key 4B 6
Lacock Gdns. BA14: Hilp 6H 31
Ladydown BA14: Trow 2E 31
Ladymead Ho. BA1: Bath 2E 5 (2H 17)
Laggan Gdns. BA1: Bath 6F 11
Lamb Ale Grn. BA14: Trow 1F 33
Lamberts Marsh BA14: S'wick 5A 32
Lambourn Rd. BS31: Key 3F 7
LAMBRIDGE .6B 12
Lambridge Bldgs. BA1: Bath 5A 12
Lambridge Bldgs. M. BA1: Bath 6B 12
    (off Salisbury Rd.)
Lambridge Grange BA1: Bath 5B 12
Lambridge M. BA1: Bath 6B 12
Lambridge Pl. BA1: Bath 6B 12
Lambridge St. BA1: Bath 5B 12
    (not continuous)
Lambrok Cl. BA14: Trow 1A 32
Lambrok Rd. BA14: Trow 1A 32
Lamont Ho. BA1: Bath 5B 12
Lampards Bldgs. BA1: Bath 1D 4 (1G 17)
Lamplighters Wlk. BA14: Trow 6D 30
Landseer Rd. BA2: Bath 3C 16
Langdon Rd. BA2: Bath 5C 16
Langford Rd. BA14: Trow 3D 30
Langford's La. BS39: High L 3E 39
Langley Down La. BA3: Mid N 3A 44
Langley Rd. BA14: Trow 2D 32
Langley's La. BA3: Clapt, Mid N 6A 44
    BS39: Paul 6A 44
Langridge La. BA1: L'rdge, L'dwn 1C 10
Langton Ct. BA2: New L 4E 15
LANSDOWN .1C 10
Lansdown (Park & Ride) 2D 10

Lansdown Cl. BA1: Bath 6F **11**
BA14: Trow 6C **30**
Lansdown Cres. BA1: Bath 6G **11**
BA2: Tim 1C **40**
Lansdown Gro. BA1: Bath 1D **4** (1G **17**)
Lansdown Gro. Ct. *BA1: Bath 1G 17*
(off Lansdown Gro.)
Lansdown Hgts. BA1: Bath 5G **11**
Lansdown La. BA1: L'dwn, W'ton 5C **10**
Lansdown Lawn Tennis & Squash Racquets Club **6G 11**
Lansdown Mans. *BA1: Bath 1G 17*
(off Lansdown Rd.)
Lansdown M. BA1: Bath 3D **4** (2G **17**)
Lansdown Pk. BA1: L'dwn 4F **11**
Lansdown Pl. BS39: High L 2E **39**
Lansdown Pl. E. BA1: Bath 1G **17**
Lansdown Pl. W. BA1: Bath 6G **11**
Lansdown Rd. BA1: Bath 1D **4** (1G **17**)
BA1: L'dwn 1C **10**
BS31: Salt 4B **8**
Lansdown Ter. *BA1: Bath 1D 4*
(off Lansdown Rd.)
BA1: W'ton 6D **10**
Lansdown Vw. BA2: Bath 3D **16**
BA2: Tim 1C **40**
Larch Ct. BA3: Rads 5H **45**
Larch Gro. BA14: Trow 1C **32**
Larchwood Ct. BA3: Rads 2C **46**
Lark Cl. BA3: Mid N 5F **45**
Larkdown BA14: Trow 4F **31**
LARKHALL **5A 12**
Larkhall Bldgs. *BA1: Bath 5B 12*
(off St Saviours Rd.)
Larkhall Pl. BA1: Bath 5B **12**
Larkhall Sq. BA1: Bath 5B **12**
Larkhall Ter. BA1: Bath 5B **12**
Lark Pl. *BA1: Bath 2E 17*
(off Up. Bristol Rd.)
Larkrise BA14: Trow 6G **31**
Larkspur BA14: Trow 4F **31**
Late Broads BA15: W'ley 4A **24**
Laura Pl. BA2: Bath 3F **5** (2H **17**)
Laurel Dr. BS39: Paul 6F **39**
Laurel Gdns. BA2: Tim 2B **40**
Laurel Gro. BA14: Trow 1D **32**
Laurels, The BA2: Mid 6B **22**
BA15: West 2C **28**
Lavender Cl. BA14: Trow 6F **31**
Lawson Cl. BS31: Salt 5H **7**
Laxton Way BA2: Pea J 4B **42**
Lays Dr. BS31: Key 2B **6**
Lays Farm Bus. Cen. BS31: Key 3B **6**
Lays Farm Trad. Est. BS31: Key 3B **6**
Leafield Pl. BA14: Trow 4A **30**
Leap Ga. BA14: Hilp 4H **31**
Leaze, The BA3: Rads 5H **45**
Leigh Cl. BA1: Bath 5H **11**
LEIGH GROVE **2H 25**
Leigh Pk. Rd. BA15: Brad A 3G **25**
Leigh Rd. BA14: Holt 1D **26**
BA15: Brad L, Brad A 3H **25**
Leigh Rd. W. BA15: Brad A 2F **25**
Leighton Rd. BA1: W'ton 4B **10**
Leopold Bldgs. BA1: Bath 1E **5**
Leslie Ri. BA15: West 2C **28**
Lewis Ct. BA14: S'wick 5B **32**
Liddington Way BA14: Trow 2E **33**
Lilac Ct. BS31: Key 4B **6**
Lilac Gro. BA14: Trow 2C **32**
Lilac Ter. BA3: Mid N 3G **45**
Lilian Ter. BS39: Paul 6G **39**
Lillington Cl. BA3: Rads 3D **46**
Lillington Rd. BA3: Rads 3D **46**
Lilliput Ct. *BA1: Bath 5E 5*
(off North Pde. Pas.)
Limeburn Hill BS40: Chew M 2C **34**
Lime Ct. BS31: Key 3B **6**
Lime Gro. BA2: Bath 5G **5** (3A **18**)
Lime Gro. Gdns. BA2: Bath 5G **5** (3A **18**)
Limekiln La. BA2: C'ton D 5E **19**
Limekilns Cl. BS31: Key 2E **7**
Lime Ter. BA3: Rads 4H **45**
LIMPLEY STOKE **5F 23**
Limpley Stoke Rd. BA15: W'ley 4H **23**
Lincoln Cl. BS31: Key 3B **6**
Lincombe Rd. BA3: Rads 5H **45**
Lincott Vw. BA2: Pea J 3A **42**
Linden Cl. BA3: Rads 5A **46**
Linden Cres. BA15: West 2D **28**
Linden Gdns. BA1: W'ton 1E **17**
Linden Pl. BA14: Trow 4C **30**
Lindisfarne Cl. BA15: W'ley 4B **24**
Linen Wlk. BA1: Swa 5B **12**
Linley Cl. BA2: Bath 4B **16**
Linleys, The BA1: Bath 2D **16**
Linne Ho. BA2: Bath 4B **16**
Linnet Way BA3: Mid N 5F **45**
Lions Orchard BA14: Holt 3F **27**
Lippiatt La. BA2: Tim 1B **40**
Lister Gro. BA15: West 2C **28**
LITTLE ASHLEY **2D 24**
Littlebrook BA14: Stav 6E **27**
BS39: Paul 5G **39**
Little Comn. BA14: N Bra 4E **33**
Little Hill BA2: Bath 3B **16**
Little Parks BA14: Holt 2G **27**
LITTLE SOLSBURY **3D 12**
Little Solsbury Hill Fort **3C 12**
Lit. Stanhope St. BA1: Bath 4B **4** (3F **17**)
Little Theatre Cinema **5D 4**
LITTLETON **1A 34**
Littleton La. BA2: Ston L, Wel 5F **43**
BS40: Chew M, Winf 1B **34**
Livingstone Rd. BA2: Bath 4E **17**
Livingstone Ter. BA2: Bath 6A **4**
Lockeridge Cl. BA14: Trow 2E **33**
Lockingwell Rd. BS31: Key 2B **6**
Locksbrook Ct. BA1: Bath 3C **16**
Locksbrook Pl. BA1: Bath 2D **16**
Locksbrook Rd. BA1: Bath 3C **16**
Locksbrook Rd. Trad. Est. BA1: Bath . . . 3C **16**
Loddon Way BA15: Brad A 6H **25**
Lodge Ct. BA14: Trow 5F **31**
Lodge Gdns. BA2: Odd D 2E **21**
London Rd. BA1: Bath 1E **5** (1H **17**)
London Rd. E. BA1: Bathe, Bathf 4E **13**
London Rd. W. BA1: Bath, Bathe 6B **12**
London St. BA1: Bath 1E **5** (1H **17**)
Long Acre BA1: Bath 1H **17**
Longacre Ho. BA1: Bath 1H **17**
Long Barnaby BA3: Mid N 3E **45**
Longfellow Av. BA2: Bath 5G **17**
Longfellow Rd. BA3: Rads 5G **45**
LONGFIELD **6E 31**
Longfield Rd. BA14: Trow 5E **31**
(not continuous)
Long Hay Cl. BA2: Bath 4C **16**
Longmeadow Rd. BS31: Key 3B **6**
Longreach BS31: Salt 3H **7**
Longs Yd. BA15: Brad A 5G **25**
Longthorne Pl. BA2: C Down 1G **21**
Long Valley Rd. BA2: Bath 4A **16**
Longvernal BA3: Mid N 4D **44**
Loop Rd. BA1: Bath 3E **5** (2H **17**)
Lorne Rd. BA2: Bath 5A **4** (3E **17**)
Lotmead BA14: Stav 6E **27**
Lovers La. BS39: Paul 1E **45**
Love's Hill BA2: Tim 2A **40**
Loves La. BA2: F'boro 3G **37**
BA14: Wing 6F **29**
Lwr. Alma St. BA14: Trow 5F **31**
Lower Batch BS40: Chew M 2F **35**
Lwr. Borough Walls
BA1: Bath 5D **4** (3G **17**)
Lwr. Bristol Rd. BA2: Bath 4A **4** (1H **15**)
BS39: Clut 6B **36**
Lwr. Camden Pl. BA1: Bath 1H **17**
Lower Ct. BA14: Trow 3E **31**
Lwr. East Hayes BA1: Bath 1A **18**
Lwr. Farm La. BA2: Cor 2E **15**
Lwr. Hedgemead Rd.
BA1: Bath 1E **5** (1H **17**)
Lower Northend BA1: Bathe 2E **13**
Lwr. Oldfield Pk. BA2: Bath 6A **4** (4E **17**)
LOWER PEASEDOWN **3H 41**
Lower Stoke BA2: Lim S 2F **23**
LOWER STUDLEY **1E 33**
LOWER SWAINSWICK **5B 12**
LOWER WESTON **2D 16**
LOWER WESTWOOD **2D 28**
Lower Westwood BA15: West 3B **28**
Lower Whitelands BA3: Rads 2D **46**
LOWER WRITHLINGTON **2E 47**
Lowmead BA14: Trow 4F **31**
Loxley Gdns. BA2: Bath 5D **16**
Loxton Dr. BA2: Bath 3C **16**
Luccombe Quarry BA15: Brad A 4H **25**
Lucklands Rd. BA1: W'ton 6D **10**
Ludlow Cl. BS31: Key 2C **6**
Ludwells Orchard BS39: Paul 6G **39**
Luke's Cl. BA3: Rads 2B **46**
Lulworth Rd. BS31: Key 3D **6**
Lyddieth Ct. BA15: W'ley 4B **24**
Lydiard Way BA14: Trow 2E **33**
LYE GREEN **1D 28**
Lyme Gdns. BA1: Bath 2C **16**
Lyme Rd. BA1: Bath 2C **16**
Lymore Av. BA2: Bath 4D **16**
Lymore Cl. BA2: Bath 5D **16**
Lymore Gdns. BA2: Bath 4D **16**
Lymore Ter. BA2: Bath 5D **16**
Lympsham Grn. BA2: Odd D 2E **21**
Lynbrook La. BA2: Bath 6G **17**
LYNCOMBE HILL **5H 17**
Lyncombe Hill BA2: Bath 6F **5** (4H **17**)
LYNCOMBE VALE **6H 17**
Lyncombe Va. BA2: Bath 5H **17**
Lyncombe Va. Rd. BA2: Bath 6H **17**
Lyndhurst Bungs. BA15: Brad A 5G **25**
Lyndhurst Pl. BA1: Bath 1H **17**
Lyndhurst Rd. BA2: Bath 3D **16**
BA3: Mid N 5F **45**
BS31: Key 4E **7**
Lyndhurst Ter. BA1: Bath 1H **17**
Lyneham Way BA14: Trow 5G **31**
Lynfield Pk. BA1: W'ton 5D **10**
Lynton Rd. BA3: Mid N 5F **45**
Lynwood Cl. BA3: Mid N 5E **45**
Lynwood Dr. BA14: Trow 4B **30**
Lytes Cary Rd. BS31: Key 5F **7**
Lytton Gdns. BA2: Bath 5C **16**
Lytton Gro. BS31: Key 2F **7**

M

Macaulay Bldgs. BA2: Bath 5B **18**
McDonogh Ct. BA14: Trow 5F **31**
Macies, The BA1: W'ton 4C **10**
Madam's Paddock BS40: Chew M 3F **35**
Maddocks Rd. BA14: Stav 1E **31**
Maesbury Rd. BS31: Key 5F **7**
Magdalen Av. BA2: Bath 6C **4** (4G **17**)
Magdalene Rd. BA3: Writ 3E **47**
Magdalen La. BA14: Wing 6E **29**
Magdalen Rd. BA2: Bath 6C **4** (4G **17**)
Maggs Hill BA2: Tim 1B **40**
Magistrates' Court
Bath 4G 5 (3A 18)
Magnolia Ri. BA14: Trow 6F **31**
Magnolia Rd. BA3: Rads 4A **46**
Magnon Rd. BA15: Brad A 4E **25**
Mallard Cl. BA14: Trow 6F **31**
Mallow Cl. BA14: Trow 1E **33**
Maltings, The BA15: Brad A 6G **25**
Maltings Ind. Est., The BA1: Bath 2B **16**
Maltings, Ind. Pk., The
BA14: Trow 4C **30**
Malvern Bldgs. BA1: Bath 5H **11**
Malvern Ter. BA1: Bath 6H **11**
Malvern Vs. *BA1: Bath 6H 11*
(off Camden Rd.)
Malwayn Cl. BA14: Hilp 4G **31**
Mandy Mdws. BA3: Mid N 4D **44**
Manley Cl. BA14: Trow 4D **30**

Manor Cl. BA2: F'frd 6H **23**
BA2: Wel 2H **43**
BA14: Trow 1B **32**
Mnr. Copse Rd. BA3: Writ 3E **47**
Manor Ct. BA14: Trow 1B **32**
Manor Dr. BA1: Bathf 5H **13**
Mnr. Farm Cl. BS39: Paul 5F **39**
Manor Gdns. BA2: F'boro 3H **37**
Manor Pk. BA1: Bath 1C **16**
BA3: Writ 3E **47**
Manor Pk. Cl. BA3: Writ 3E **47**
Manor Rd. BA1: W'ton 6D **10**
BA3: Writ 3E **47**
BA14: Trow 1B **32**
BS31: Key, Salt 4E **7**
Manor Ter. BA3: Writ 3E **47**
Manor Vs. BA1: W'ton 6D **10**
Mansbrook Ho. BA3: Mid N 4E **45**
Mansel Cl. BS31: Salt 4H **7**
Manton Cl. BA14: Trow 2D **32**
Manvers St. BA1: Bath 5F **5** (3H **17**)
BA14: Trow 4E **31**
Maple Dr. BA3: Rads 4A **46**
Maple Gdns. BA2: Bath 5F **17**
Maple Gro. BA2: Bath 5F **17**
BA14: Trow 1D **32**
Maple Ri. BA3: Rads 3D **46**
Maple Wlk. BS31: Key 3C **6**
Marden Rd. BS31: Key 3F **7**
Marden Wlk. BA14: Trow 1E **33**
Margaret's Bldgs.
BA1: Bath 2C **4** (2G **17**)
Margaret's Hill
BA1: Bath 1E **5** (1H **17**)
Margaret's St. BA15: Brad A 5G **25**
Marina Dr. BA14: Stav 1E **31**
Market Pl. BA3: Rads 2B **46**
Market St. BA14: Trow 5E **31**
BA15: Brad A 4G **25**
Marlborough Bldgs.
BA1: Bath 2B **4** (2F **17**)
Marlborough Ct. BA2: C'ton D 3D **18**
Marlborough La. BA1: Bath 3B **4** (2F **17**)
Marlborough St. BA1: Bath 1B **4** (1F **17**)
Marsden Rd. BA2: Bath 6C **16**
Marshfield Way BA1: Bath 6H **11**
Marsh La. BS39: Clut, Hall 1B **38**
Marshmead BA14: Hilp 1G **31**
Marsh Rd. BA14: Hilp 6F **27**
Marston Rd. BA14: Trow 2C **32**
Martock Rd. BS31: Key 4F **7**
Masons La. BA15: Brad A 4G **25**
Maulton Cl. BA14: Holt 3E **27**
Maunders Dr. BA14: Stav 1E **31**
Maxcroft La. BA14: Hilp 6F **27**
Maybrick Rd. BA2: Bath 4E **17**
Mayfield Rd. BA2: Bath 4E **17**
Mayfields BS31: Key 2D **6**
May La. BA1: Bath 1C **16**
Maynard Ter. BS39: Clut 6B **36**
Maypole Cl. BS39: Clut 6A **36**
May Tree Rd. BA3: Rads 4A **46**
May Tree Wlk. BS31: Key 4B **6**
Mead, The BA2: F'boro 3H **37**
BA2: Tim 1C **40**
BA15: W'ley 4B **24**
BS39: Clut 6A **36**
(not continuous)
BS39: Paul 6F **39**
Mead Cl. BA2: Bath 6F **17**
Mead Ct. BA14: N Bra 4E **33**
Meade Ho. BA2: Bath 4B **16**
MEADGATE EAST 1E **41**
MEADGATE WEST 1D **40**
Meadlands BA2: Cor 2E **15**
Mead La. BS31: Salt 3C **8**
Meadow Ct. BA1: Bath 2B **16**
BA14: Stav 1E **31**
Meadow Dr. BA2: Odd D 3E **21**
Meadowfield BA15: Brad A 5E **25**
Meadow Gdns. BA1: Bath 6B **10**
Meadow La. BA2: Batham 6C **12**
Meadow Lea BS39: Hall 5C **38**
Meadow Pk. BA1: Bathf 4G **13**
Meadow Rd. BS39: Paul 1D **44**
Meadow Vw. BA3: Rads 4C **46**
BA14: S'wick 3A **32**
Meadow Vw. Cl. BA1: Bath 1B **16**
Meadow Works BA14: Trow 5D **30**
Meadway BA14: Trow 5B **30**
BS39: Temp C 2A **38**
Meare Rd. BA2: C Down 1G **21**
MEARNS 1G **39**
Medway Cl. BS31: Key 4F **7**
Medway Dr. BS31: Key 4F **7**
Melcombe Ct. BA2: Bath 5E **17**
Melcombe Rd. BA2: Bath 4E **17**
Melksham Rd. BA14: Holt 2G **27**
Mells Cl. BS31: Key 5F **7**
Mells La. BA3: Rads 3D **46**
Melrose Gro. BA2: Bath 6C **16**
Melrose Ter. BA1: Bath 5H **11**
Melton Rd. BA14: Trow 3D **30**
Memorial Cotts. BA1: W'ton 6D **10**
Mendip Cl. BS31: Key 2C **6**
BS39: Paul 1C **44**
Mendip Gdns. BA2: Odd D 3E **21**
Mendip Way BA3: Rads 2B **46**
Meriden BA1: W'ton 1E **17**
Meridian Bus. Pk.
BA14: N Bra 4F **33**
Meridian Wlk. BA14: Trow 5B **30**
Methuen Cl. BA15: Brad A 1H **29**
Mews, The BA1: Bath 1B **16**
Mezellion Pl. *BA1: Bath* *6A* ***12***
(off Camden Rd.)
Michaels Mead BA1: W'ton 5C **10**
Michael Tippett Cen., The 4E **15**
Middle La. BA1: Bath 6A **12**
BA14: Hilp, Trow 3G **31**
Middlepiece La. BS31: Burn 2A **14**
Middle Rank BA15: Brad A 4F **25**
Middle Stoke BA2: Lim S 5E **23**
Middlewood Cl. BA2: Odd D 1D **20**
MIDFORD 5A **22**
Midford Hill BA2: Mid 5B **22**
Midford La. BA2: Lim S, Mid 5B **22**
Midford Rd.
BA2: C Down, Odd D, S'ske 2F **21**
BA2: Mid, S'ske 3H **21**
Midland Bri. Rd. BA1: Bath 5B **4** (3F **17**)
BA2: Bath 5B **4** (3F **17**)
Midland Rd. BA1: Bath 2E **17**
BA2: Bath 3A **4** (3E **17**)
Midlands, The BA14: Holt 3F **27**
Midlands Ind. Est. BA14: Holt 2F **27**
Midsomer Ent. Pk.
BA3: Mid N 3G **45**
MIDSOMER NORTON 4E **45**
Midsomer Norton South Station
Somerset & Dorset Railway Heritage Trust
5E **45**
Midsummer Bldgs. BA1: Bath 5A **12**
Miles's Bldgs. BA1: Bath 3D **4** (2G **17**)
Miles St. BA2: Bath 6F **5** (4H **17**)
Milk St. BA1: Bath 5D **4** (3G **17**)
Mill, The BS39: Hall 3C **38**
Millards Cl. BA14: Hilp 1G **31**
Millards Ct. BA3: Mid N 2F **45**
Millard's Hill BA3: Mid N 2F **45**
Millbourn Cl. BA15: W'ley 4A **24**
Millbrook Ct. *BA2: Bath* *4H* ***17***
(off Millbrook Pl.)
Millbrook La. BA2: Bath 6F **5** (4H **17**)
Millbrook Pl. BA2: Bath 6F **5** (4H **17**)
Mill Ct. BA3: Mid N 4E **45**
Miller Wlk. BA2: Batham 6D **12**
Millfield BA3: Mid N 5D **44**
Millhand Vs. BA14: Trow 1F **33**
Mill Hill BA2: Wel 2H **43**
Mill Ho., The BA15: Brad A 5G **25**
Millington Dr. BA14: Trow 6B **30**
Mill La. BA2: Bath 3C **16**
BA2: Batham 5E **13**
Mill La. BA2: Mon C 3D **22**
BA2: Tim 2B **40**
BA3: Rads 2D **46**
BA15: Brad A 5G **25**
BS40: Chew S 5B **34**
Millmead Rd. BA2: Bath 4D **16**
Mill Rd. BA3: Rads 3C **46**
Mill Rd. Ind. Est. BA3: Rads 2C **46**
Mill St. BA14: Trow 5E **31**
Millward Ter. BS39: Paul 5G **39**
Milsom Pl. BA1: Bath 3D **4** (2G **17**)
Milsom St.
BA1: Bath 3D **4** (2G **17**)
Milton Av. BA2: Bath 5G **17**
Milton Rd. BA3: Rads 4G **45**
Milward Rd. BS31: Key 1D **6**
Miner's Gdns. BA3: Rads 3A **46**
Minerva Ct. BA2: Bath 2F **5** (2H **17**)
Minerva Gdns. BA2: Bath 4D **16**
Minsmere Rd. BS31: Key 4F **7**
Minster Way BA2: Bath 1B **18**
Mission Theatre, The 5D **4**
Mitre Ct. *BA14: Trow* *4E* ***31***
(off Duke St.)
Molly Cl. BS39: Temp C 3A **38**
MONGER 2D **44**
Monger Cotts. BS39: Paul 2E **45**
Monger La. BA3: Mid N 2D **44**
BS39: Paul 2D **44**
Monksdale Rd. BA2: Bath 5E **17**
MONKTON COMBE 2D **22**
Monmouth Ct. *BA1: Bath* *4B* ***4***
(off Up. Bristol Rd.)
Monmouth Pl. BA1: Bath 4C **4** (3G **17**)
Monmouth Rd. BS31: Key 2C **6**
Monmouth St. BA1: Bath 4C **4** (3G **17**)
Montague Ct. BA14: Hilp 4H **31**
Montague Rd. BA2: Shos 6C **42**
BS31: Salt 5H **7**
Montpelier BA1: Bath 2D **4** (2G **17**)
Montrose Cotts. BA1: W'ton 6D **10**
Moorfields Cl. BA2: Bath 5E **17**
Moorfields Dr. BA2: Bath 5E **17**
Moorfields Rd. BA2: Bath 5E **17**
Moorhen Cl. BA14: Stav 1E **31**
Moorland Rd. BA2: Bath 4E **17**
MOORLANDS 5E **17**
Moorlands, The BA2: Bath 6E **17**
MOORLEDGE 4H **35**
Moorledge La. BS40: Chew M 4G **35**
Moorledge Rd. BS40: Chew M 3F **35**
MOORSFIELD 6A **36**
Morford St. BA1: Bath 2D **4** (1G **17**)
Morgan Cl. BS31: Salt 5A **8**
Morgan Way BA2: Pea J 4B **42**
Morley Ter. BA2: Bath 3E **17**
BA3: Rads 2C **46**
Morris Cl. BA1: Bathf 4G **13**
Morris La. BA1: Bathf 4G **13**
Mortimer Cl. BA1: W'ton 5C **10**
Mortimer St. BA14: Trow 6D **30**
Moulton Dr. BA15: Brad A 1G **29**
Mount, The BA14: Trow 3E **31**
Mountain Ash BA1: W'ton 6E **11**
Mountain's La. BA2: F'boro 2F **37**
Mountain Wood BA1: Bathf 5H **13**
Mount Beacon BA1: Bath 6H **11**
Mt. Beacon Pl. BA1: Bath 6G **11**
Mt. Beacon Row BA1: Bath 6H **11**
Mount Gro. BA2: Bath 6C **16**
Mt. Pleasant BA2: Mon C 2C **22**
BA3: Rads 3D **46**
BA15: Brad A 4G **25**
Mount Rd. BA1: Bath 1G **17**
BA2: Bath 5B **16**
Mount Vw. *BA1: Bath* *6H* ***11***
(off Beacon Rd.)
BA2: Bath 6C **16**
Moyle Pk. BA14: Hilp 4H **31**
MURHILL 5H **23**
Murray Rd. BA14: Trow 3E **31**
Mus. of Bath at Work 1D **4** (1G **17**)

Mus. of East Asian Art 2C 4 (2G 17)
Mythern Mdw. BA15: Brad A 6H 25

N

Naishes Av. BA2: Pea J 3B 42
Naish Ho. BA2: Bath 3B 16
Napier La. BA1: W'ton 4B 10
Narrow Wine St. BA14: Trow 5E 31
　　　　　(off Market St.)
Nash Cl. BS31: Key 2F 7
Nasmilco Ter. BA14: Stav 5E 27
Navigator Cl. BA14: Trow 1F 31
Nelson Bldgs. BA1: Bath 1F 5 (1H 17)
Nelson Ho. BA1: Bath 3B 4 (2F 17)
Nelson Pl. E. BA1: Bath 1E 5 (1H 17)
Nelson Pl. W. BA1: Bath 4B 4 (3F 17)
Nelson Vs. BA1: Bath 4A 4 (3F 17)
Nestings, The BA14: Trow 2B 32
Nevill Ct. BA2: New L 4E 15
Newark St. BA1: Bath 6E 5 (4H 17)
New Bond St. BA1: Bath 4D 4 (3G 17)
New Bond St. Bldgs. BA1: Bath 4D 4
　　　　　(off New Bond St.)
New Bond St. Pl. BA1: Bath 4E 5
NEWBRIDGE 1B 16
Newbridge (Park & Ride) 1A 16
Newbridge Ct. BA1: Bath 2C 16
Newbridge Gdns. BA1: Bath 1B 16
Newbridge Hill BA1: Bath 1B 16
Newbridge Rd. BA1: Bath 1H 15
　　BA2: Bath 1H 15
NEW BUILDINGS 4G 41
Newhurst Pk. BA14: Hilp 3H 31
New King St. BA1: Bath 4B 4 (3G 17)
Newlands Rd. BS31: Key 3C 6
Newleaze BA14: Hilp 1G 31
Newmans La. BA2: Tim 1B 40
New Marchants Pas.
　　BA1: Bath 6E 5 (4H 17)
Newmarket Av. BA14: Trow 3F 33
Newmarket Row BA2: Bath 4E 5
　　　　　(off Grand Pde.)
New Orchard St. BA1: Bath 5E 5 (3H 17)
New Pit BS39: Paul 5H 39
New Rd. BA1: Bathf 5H 13
　　BA2: F'frd 6G 23
　　BA2: Tim 6F 37
　　BA14: Trow 6E 31
　　　　　(not continuous)
　　BA15: Brad A 4G 25
　　BS39: High L 1E 39
New Rd. Ct. BA15: Brad A 4H 25
New St. BA1: Bath 5D 4 (3G 17)
New Ter. BA14: Hilp, Stav 5E 27
Newton Mill Camping & Cvn. Pk.
　　BA2: New L 3H 15
Newton Pk. 3E 15
Newton Rd. BA2: Bath 4A 16
NEWTON ST LOE 3G 15
NEWTOWN 6H 35
Newtown BA14: Trow 5D 30
　　BA15: Brad A 5F 25
　　BS39: Paul 6F 39
New Tyning Ter. BA1: Bath 6A 12
　　　　　(off Fairfield Rd.)
New Villas BA2: Bath 5H 17
NHS WALK-IN CENTRE (BATH)
　　. . . . . .4B 4 (3F 17)
Nibbs Ter. BA14: Holt 2F 27
Nicholl's Pl. BA1: Bath 2D 4
　　　　　(off Lansdown Rd.)
Nightingale Rd. BA14: Trow 5B 30
Nightingale Way BA3: Mid N 5F 45
Nile St. BA1: Bath 4B 4 (3F 17)
Norfolk Bldgs. BA1: Bath 4B 4 (3F 17)
Norfolk Cres. BA1: Bath 4B 4 (3F 17)
Norfolk Gro. BS31: Key 3B 6
Norman Rd. BS31: Salt 4A 8
Normans, The BA2: Batham 6E 13
Norris Rd. BA14: Hilp 5H 31

Northampton Bldgs.
　　BA1: Bath 1C 4 (1G 17)
Northampton St. BA1: Bath 1C 4 (1G 17)
Northanger Ct. BA2: Bath 3E 5
　　　　　(off Grove St.)
NORTH BRADLEY 4E 33
Nth. Chew Ter. BS40: Chew M 2F 35
Northdown Rd. BA3: Clan 6E 41
NORTH END
　　BA1 . . . . .2E 13
　　BS39 . . . . .4A 36
Northend BA3: Mid N 3F 45
Northend Cotts. BA1: Bathe 2E 13
NORTHFIELD 3D 46
Northfield BA3: Rads 2C 46
　　BA15: W'ley 4C 24
Northfields BA1: Bath 6G 11
Northfields Cl. BA1: Bath 6G 11
Northgate St. BA1: Bath 4E 5 (3H 17)
Northgate Yd. BA1: Bath 4E 5
　　　　　(off Northgate St.)
North La. BA2: C'ton D 4C 18
Northleigh BA15: Brad A 2H 25
Northmead Av. BA3: Mid N 3D 44
Northmead Cl. BA3: Mid N 3D 44
North Mdws. BA2: Pea J 3B 42
Northmead Rd. BA3: Mid N 3D 44
North Pde. BA1: Bath 5F 5 (3H 17)
　　BA2: Bath 5F 5 (3H 17)
North Pde. Bldgs. BA1: Bath 5E 5
　　　　　(off Abbeygate St.)
North Pde. Pas. BA1: Bath 5E 5 (3H 17)
North Pde. Rd. BA2: Bath 5F 5 (3H 17)
North Rd. BA2: Bath, C'ton D 2H 5 (2B 18)
　　BA2: C Down 2A 22
　　BA2: Tim 1B 40
　　BA3: Mid N 4D 44
NORTH STOKE 1F 9
Northumberland Bldgs. BA1: Bath 4D 4
　　　　　(off Barton St.)
Northumberland Pl. BA1: Bath . . .4E 5 (3H 17)
North Vw. BA2: Pea J 3A 42
　　BA3: Rads 3D 46
North Vw. Cl. BA2: Bath 4C 16
North Way BA2: Bath 4B 16
　　BA3: Mid N 4E 45
Norton Cl. BS40: Chew M 2F 35
NORTON HILL 5F 45
Norton Hill Sports Cen. 6F 45
Norton La. BS40: Chew M 1F 35
Norwood Av. BA2: C'ton D 5D 18
Norwood Ct. BA14: Trow 4D 30
　　　　　(off Wicker Hill)
No. 1 Royal Crescent 2B 4 (2F 17)
Nunney Cl. BS31: Key 5F 7
Nursery Cl. BA14: Hilp 2H 31
Nutgrove La. BS40: Chew M 2E 35

O

Oak Av. BA2: Bath 6D 16
Oak Dr. BA14: N Bra 4D 32
Oakfield Cl. BA1: Bath 1E 17
Oakfield Rd. BS31: Key 4E 7
Oakford La. BA1: Bathe 1F 13
Oakhill Rd. BA2: C Down 1G 21
Oaklands BS39: Paul 1C 44
　　BS39: Temp C 2A 38
Oakley BA2: C'ton D 4D 18
Oak St. BA2: Bath 6C 4 (4G 17)
Oak Ter. BA3: Rads 4H 45
Oak Tree Cl. BA14: Trow 4C 30
Oak Tree Wlk. BS31: Key 3C 6
Oakwood Gdns. BA2: C'ton D 4C 18
Oatfields BA14: Stav 1E 31
ODD DOWN 2E 21
Odd Down (Park & Ride) 3D 20
Odeon Cinema
　　Bath 5C 4 (3G 17)
Odins Rd. BA2: Odd D 2E 21
Office Village, The BA2: Pea J 4C 42

Old Batch, The BA15: Brad A 3E 25
Old Bond St. BA1: Bath 4D 4 (3G 17)
Oldbrick Flds. BA14: Trow 2B 32
Old Bristol Rd. BS31: Key 1B 6
Old Ct. BA15: Brad A 5H 25
Old Dairy, The BA2: Bath 5E 17
Old England Way BA2: Pea J 3B 42
Old Farm Rd. BA14: Trow 6G 31
Old Ferry Rd. BA2: Bath 3D 16
Oldfield La. BA2: Bath 5E 17
OLDFIELD PARK 6A 4 (4F 17)
Oldfield Park Station (Rail) 3E 17
Oldfield Pl. BA2: Bath 6B 4 (4F 17)
Oldfield Rd. BA2: Bath 4F 17
Old Forge Way BA2: Pea J 3C 42
Old Fosse Rd. BA2: Odd D 1D 20
　　BA3: Clan 1A 46
Old Frome Rd. BA2: Odd D 3F 21
Old King St. BA1: Bath 3D 4 (2G 17)
Old Midford Rd. BA2: S'ske 4H 21
Old Mill, The BA14: Trow 5F 31
Old Millard's Hill BA3: Mid N 2F 45
OLD MILLS 2B 44
Old Mills Ind. Est.
　　BS39: Paul 3C 44
Old Mills La. BS39: Paul 2B 44
Old Newbridge Hill
　　BA1: Bath 1B 16
Old Orchard BA1: Bath 2E 5 (2H 17)
Old Orchard St. BA1: Bath 5E 5 (3H 17)
Old Pit Rd. BA3: Mid N 5F 45
Old Pit Ter. BA3: Clan 1A 46
Old Quarry BA2: Odd D 1E 21
Old Rd. BA3: Writ 4E 47
Old School, The BA1: Bath 1C 4
Old School Hill BA2: S'ske 4G 21
Old Station Bus. Pk.
　　BS39: Hall 4C 38
Old Track BA2: Lim S 4E 23
Old Vicarage Grn. BS31: Key 1D 6
Old Wells Rd. BA2: Bath 6G 17
Oliver Brooks Rd. BA3: Mid N 6C 44
Onega Cen. BA1: Bath 3A 4
Onega Ter. BA1: Bath 3A 4 (2F 17)
Oolite Gro. BA2: Odd D 2E 21
Oolite Rd. BA2: Odd D 2E 21
Orange Gro. BA1: Bath 4E 5 (3H 17)
Orchard, The BA2: C Down 2A 22
　　BA2: Cor 1E 15
　　BA2: F'frd 6H 23
Orchard Av. BA3: Mid N 4D 44
Orchard Cl. BA15: West 2C 28
　　BS31: Key 1B 6
Orchard Ct. BA14: Trow 6E 31
Orchard Dr. BA14: S'wick 4A 32
Orchard Gdns. BA15: Brad A 5G 25
　　　　　(off Up. Regents Pk.)
　　BS39: Paul 5G 39
Orchard Lodge BA2: Batham 1E 19
Orchard Rd. BA14: Trow 6E 31
　　BS39: Paul 5G 39
Orchard Ter. BA2: Bath 3C 16
Orchard Va. BA3: Mid N 4C 44
Orchard Way BA2: Pea J 4B 42
　　BA14: N Bra 4D 32
Orchid Dr. BA2: Odd D 2D 20
Oriel Cl. BA14: Hilp 2H 31
Oriel Gdns. BA1: Swa 5B 12
Oriel Gro. BA2: Bath 5C 16
Orpington Way BA14: Hilp 4H 31
Orwell Dr. BS31: Key 3E 7
Osborne Rd. BA1: Bath 3C 16
　　BA14: Trow 2F 31
Ostlings La. BA1: Bathf 5G 13
Otago Ter. BA1: Bath 5B 12
Oval, The BA2: Bath 5D 16
OVAL, THE 5D 16
Oval, The BA2: Bath 5D 16
Overdale BA2: Tun 1F 41
　　BA3: Clan 6E 41
Oxford Gdns. BA14: Hilp 4G 31
Oxford Pl. BA2: C Down 1B 22
Oxford Row BA1: Bath 2D 4 (2G 17)

Oxford Ter. BA2: C Down 1B 22
Oxney Pl. BA2: Pea J 4A 42

P

Pack Horse La. BA2: S'ske 4G 21
Paddock, The BA2: Cor 2E 15
Paddocks, The BA2: C Down 2A 22
Paddock Woods BA2: C Down 1C 22
Padfield Cl. BA2: Bath 4C 16
PADLEIGH 1B 20
Padleigh Hill BA2: Bath 1B 20
Pagans Hill BS40: Chew M, Chew S 3B 34
Painters Mead BA14: Hilp 3H 31
Palace Yd. M. BA1: Bath 4C 4 (3G 17)
Palairet Cl. BA15: Brad A 1G 29
Palmer Dr. BA15: Brad A 3G 25
Palmer Rd. BA14: Trow 3E 31
Parade, The BA2: Bath 3C 16
BA2: C'ton D 3D 18
Paragon BA1: Bath 2E 5 (2H 17)
Park, The BS31: Key 1D 6
Park & Ride
Batheaston By-Pass 5E 13
Lansdown 2D 10
Newbridge 1A 16
Odd Down 3D 20
University of Bath 3C 18
Park Av. BA2: Bath 6C 4 (4G 17)
Park Cl. BA14: N Bra 4E 33
BS31: Key 2C 6
BS39: Paul 6F 39
PARK CORNER 6F 23
Park Gdns. BA1: Bath 1E 17
Park Ho. BA2: Bath 5F 17
Parkhouse La. BS31: Key 5B 6
(not continuous)
Parklands BA14: Trow 3E 31
BS39: High L 1F 39
Park La. BA1: Bath 1E 17
Park Mans. BA1: Bath 1B 4 (1F 17)
Park Pl. BA1: Bath 1B 4 (1F 17)
BA2: C Down 2A 22
Park Rd. BA1: Bath 2C 16
BA14: Trow 5E 31
BS31: Key 2D 6
BS39: Paul 6F 39
Park St. BA1: Bath 1B 4 (1F 17)
BA14: Trow 6D 30
Park St. M. BA1: Bath 1B 4
Park Vw. BA2: Bath 4A 4 (3E 17)
Park Way BA3: Mid N 5E 45
Parkway BA2: Cam 1E 41
Parkway La. BA2: Cam 1D 40
Parry Cl. BA2: Bath 5C 16
Parsonage La. BA1: Bath 4D 4 (3G 17)
Parsonage Rd. BA14: Hilp 4H 31
Partis College BA1: Bath 1B 16
Partis Way BA1: Bath 1B 16
Pastures, The BA15: West 2B 28
Paulmont Ri. BS39: Temp C 2A 38
Paulto' Hill BS39: Paul 5H 39
PAULTON 5G 39
Paulton La. BA2: Cam 4D 40
PAULTON MEMORIAL HOSPITAL 1D 44
Paulton Rd. BA3: Mid N 4D 44
BS39: Far G 2A 44
Paulton Swimming Pool 6G 39
Paulwood Rd. BS39: Temp C 2A 38
Pavely Gdns. BA14: Hilp 4H 31
Pavilion, The 5F 5 (3H 17)
PAXCROFT MEAD 5H 31
Paxcroft Way BA14: Trow 5G 31
Pearl Cl. BA14: Trow 3D 30
PEASEDOWN ST JOHN 4A 42
Peasedown St John By-Pass
BA2: Pea J 2C 42
Pembroke Cl. BA14: Trow 1E 33
Pembroke Ct. BA1: W'ton 6D 10
Pennard Grn. BA2: Bath 3B 16
Penn Gdns. BA1: Bath 1B 16
Penn Hill Rd. BA1: Bath, W'ton 1B 16
Penn Lea Ct. BA1: Bath 1C 16
(not continuous)
Penn Lea Rd. BA1: Bath 6B 10
Pennyquick BA2: New L 2F 15
Pennyquick Vw. BA2: Bath 3A 16
Penthouse Hill BA1: Bathe 4E 13
Pepperacre La. BA14: Trow 4G 31
Pepys Cl. BS31: Salt 5A 8
Pera Pl. BA1: Bath 1H 17
Pera Rd. BA1: Bath 1E 5 (1H 17)
Percy Pl. BA1: Bath 6A 12
Perfect Vw. BA1: Bath 6H 11
Perrin Cl. BS39: Temp C 3A 38
PERRYMEAD 6A 18
Perrymead BA2: Bath 5A 18
Perrymead Pl. BA2: Bath 5A 18
Peterside BS39: Temp C 4A 38
Peto Garden at Iford Manor, The 2B 28
Peto Gro. BA15: West 2C 28
Phase One 3A 4 (2F 17)
Pheasant Dr. BA14: Trow 1F 33
Philippa Ho. *BA2: Bath 4E 17*
(off South Av.)
Philip St. BA1: Bath 5E 5
Phillis Hill BA3: Mid N 1D 44
BS39: Paul 1D 44
Phoenix Ho. BA1: Bath 1C 4
Piccadilly Pl. BA1: Bath 6A 12
Pickwick Rd. BA1: Bath 5H 11
Pierrepont Pl. BA1: Bath 5E 5 (3H 17)
Pierrepont St. BA1: Bath 5E 5 (3H 17)
Pilgrims Way BS40: Chew S 5B 34
Pine Ct. BA3: Rads 3C 46
BS31: Key 3B 6
BS40: Chew M 2F 35
Pines Way BA2: Bath 5A 4 (3F 17)
BA3: Rads 3C 46
Pines Way Ind. Est. BA2: Bath 5B 4
Pine Wlk. BA3: Rads 4A 46
BA14: N Bra 4D 32
Pinewood Av. BA3: Mid N 4D 44
Pinewood Gro. BA3: Mid N 4D 44
Pinewood Rd. BA3: Mid N 4D 44
Pioneer Av. BA2: C Down 2G 21
PIPEHOUSE 6E 23
Pipehouse La. BA2: F'frd 6D 22
Piplar Ground BA15: Brad A 1G 29
Pippin Cl. BA2: Pea J 4B 42
Pithay, The BS39: Paul 5G 39
Pitman Av. BA14: Trow 6C 30
Pitman Ct. BA1: Bath 5B 12
BA14: Trow 1C 32
Pitman Ho. BA2: Bath 6E 17
Pitman M. BA14: Trow 5E 31
Pit Rd. BA3: Mid N 4F 45
Pitt's La. BS40: Chew M 4F 35
Pixash Bus. Cen. BS31: Key 2G 7
Pixash La. BS31: Key 2G 7
Pleasant Pl. BA1: Bathf 5H 13
Plovers Ri. BA3: Rads 2C 46
PLUMMER'S HILL 5F 39
Plumptre Cl. BS39: Paul 6G 39
Plumptre Rd. BS39: Paul 6F 39
Podgers Dr. BA1: W'ton 5C 10
Podium, The BA1: Bath 3E 5 (3H 17)
Poets Cnr. BA3: Rads 5G 45
Polebarn Cir. BA14: Trow 5E 31
Polebarn Gdns. BA14: Trow 4E 31
Polebarn Rd. BA14: Trow 4E 31
Pomeroy La. BA14: Wing 6E 29
Pool Barton BS31: Key 1D 6
Poole Ho. BA2: Bath 4A 16
Poolemead Rd. BA2: Bath 4A 16
Poor Hill BA2: F'boro 3H 37
Pope Ct. BA2: New L 4E 15
Popes Wlk. BA2: Bath 5A 18
Poplar Cl. BA2: Bath 5E 17
Poplar Rd. BA2: Odd D 3E 21
Poplars, The BA14: Trow 2B 32
Porlock Rd. BA2: C Down 2H 21
Portland Pl. BA1: Bath 1C 4 (1G 17)
Portland Rd. BA1: Bath 1C 4
Portland Ter. *BA1: Bath 1C 4*
(off Harley St.)
Poston Way BA15: W'ley 4B 24
Potts Cl. BA1: Bathe 3E 13
Poulton BA15: Brad A 6G 25
Poulton La. BA15: Brad A 1G 29
Pound Farm Cl. BA14: Hilp 1F 31
Pound La. BA15: Brad A 5F 25
Powlett Ct. BA2: Bath 2G 5 (2A 18)
Powlett Rd. BA2: Bath 1G 5 (1A 18)
Pow's Hill BA3: Clan 1H 45
Pow's Orchard
BA3: Mid N 4E 45
Pratten Ter. BA3: Mid N 5F 45
Priddy Cl. BA2: Bath 4C 16
(not continuous)
Priest Path BS31: Q Char 4A 6
Primrose Cnr. BA14: Stav 1D 30
PRIMROSE HILL 6E 11
Primrose Hill BA1: W'ton 6E 11
Primrose La. BA3: Mid N 4F 45
Primrose Ter. BA3: Mid N 4F 45
Princes Bldgs. *BA1: Bath 3D 4*
(off George St.)
BA2: Bath 6G 5 (4A 18)
Princess Cl. BS31: Key 3D 6
Princess Gdns. BA14: Hilp 1F 31
Princes St. BA1: Bath 4D 4 (3G 17)
BA3: Clan 6E 41
Prior Pk. Bldgs. BA2: Bath 4A 18
Prior Pk. Cotts. BA2: Bath 4H 17
Prior Pk. Gdns. BA2: Bath 4A 18
Prior Pk. Landscape Garden 6B 18
Prior Pk. Rd. BA2: Bath 6G 5 (4A 18)
Priors Hill BA2: Tim 2H 39
Priory Cl. BA2: C Down 6A 18
BA3: Mid N 4E 45
BA15: Brad A 4F 25
Priory Pk. BA15: Brad A 4G 25
Priory Rd. BS31: Key 1D 6
Proby Pl. BA14: Hilp 4H 31
Prospect, The BA14: Trow 4F 31
Prospect Bldgs. BA1: Bathe 2E 13
Prospect Gdns. BA1: Bathe 2E 13
Prospect Pl. *BA1: Bath 6H 11*
(off Camden Rd.)
BA1: Bathf 5H 13
BA1: W'ton 5D 10
BA2: Bath 4G 17
BA2: C Down 2A 22
(off Combe Rd.)
BA14: Trow 4E 31
Prospect Rd. BA2: Bath 5B 18
PROVIDENCE PLACE 4D 44
Providence Pl. BA3: Mid N 4D 44
BS40: Chew S 5B 34
Pulteney Av. BA2: Bath 5G 5 (3A 18)
Pulteney Bridge 4E 5 (2H 17)
Pulteney Bri. BA2: Bath 4E 5 (3H 17)
Pulteney Ct. BA2: Bath 6G 5 (4A 18)
Pulteney Gdns. BA2: Bath 5G 5 (3A 18)
Pulteney Gro. BA2: Bath 6G 5 (4A 18)
Pulteney M. BA2: Bath 4F 5 (2H 17)
Pulteney Rd. BA2: Bath 6G 5 (4A 18)
Pulteney Ter. *BA2: Bath 5G 5*
(off Pulteney Rd.)
Pump La. BA1: Bathf 6G 13
Pump Room 4E 5 (3H 17)
Purlewent Dr. BA1: W'ton 5D 10
Purnell Way BS39: Paul 5F 39

Q

Quantocks BA2: C Down 2H 21
Quarry Cl. BA2: C Down 2G 21
BA2: Lim S 5A 24
BA15: W'ley 5A 24
Quarry Hay BS40: Chew S 5B 34
Quarrymans Ct. BA2: C Down 2A 22
Quarry Rd. BA2: C'ton D 4C 18

Quarry Rock Gdns. BA2: C'ton D 5D 18
Quarry Va. BA2: C Down 2A 22
Quarterway La. BA14: Trow 4F 31
Quebec BA2: Bath 3B 16
QUEEN CHARLTON 4A 6
Queen Charlton La. BS31: Q Char 5A 6
Queens Club Gdns. BA14: Trow 5B 30
Queen's Dr. BA2: C Down 2H 21
Queens Gdns. BA14: Hilp 1F 31
Queen's Ga. BA3: Rads 3D 46
Queens Pde. BA1: Bath 3C 4 (2G 17)
Queens Pde. Pl. BA1: Bath ...3D 4 (2G 17)
Queen Sq. BA1: Bath 6G 5 (4A 18)
Queen Sq. BA1: Bath 3D 4 (2G 17)
BS31: Salt 4C 8
Queen Sq. Pl. BA1: Bath 3C 4 (2G 17)
Queens Rd. BA3: Rads 3D 46
BA14: Trow 3D 30
BS31: Key 3C 6
Queen St. BA1: Bath 4D 4 (3G 17)
Queenwood Av. BA1: Bath 6H 11
Quiet St. BA1: Bath 4D 4 (3G 17)
Quilling Cl. BA14: Trow 6F 31

R

Raby M. BA2: Bath 3G 5 (2A 18)
Raby Pl. BA2: Bath 3G 5 (2A 18)
Raby Vs. BA2: Bath 3H 5 (2A 18)
Rackfield Pl. BA2: Bath 3C 16
Rackvernal Ct. BA3: Mid N 4F 45
Rackvernal Rd. BA3: Mid N 4F 45
RADFORD 3C 40
Radford Hill BA2: Tim 1C 40
BA3: Rads, Tim 4C 40
RADSTOCK 3B 46
Radstock Linear Pk. & Tom Huyton Play Area
....2B 46
Radstock Mus. 3B 46
Radstock Rd. BA3: Mid N 3F 45
Rag Hill BA2: Shos 6B 42
Raglan Cl. BA1: Bath 5H 11
(off Raglan La.)
Ragland La. BA1: Bath 5H 11
Raglan St. BA1: Bath 5H 11
Raglan Ter. BA1: Bath 5H 11
Raglan Vs. BA1: Bath 6H 11
Raglan Wlk. BS31: Key 3C 6
Ragleth Gro. BA14: Trow 3F 31
Railway La. BA2: Wel 2H 43
Railway Pl. BA1: Bath 6F 5 (4H 17)
Railway St. BA1: Bath 6E 5 (4H 17)
Railway Ter. BA2: Shos 1G 47
Railway Vw. Pl. BA3: Mid N 3F 45
Raleigh Cl. BS31: Salt 5H 7
Raleigh Ct. BA14: Trow 5E 31
Ralph Allen Dr. BA2: Bath, C Down ...5A 18
Rambler Cl. BA14: Trow 4B 30
Ramsbury Wlk. BA14: Trow 1E 33
Ramscombe La. BA1: Bathe 1D 12
Rank, The BA14: N Bra 4C 32
Ravenscroft Gdns. BA14: Trow 4G 31
Recreation Ground 4F 5 (3H 17)
Rectory Cl. BA2: F'boro 3H 37
Rectory La. BA2: Tim 1B 40
Redfield Gro. BA3: Mid N 4E 45
Redfield Rd. BA3: Mid N 5D 44
Redgrave Cl. BA14: Trow 1E 33
Red Hat La. BA14: Trow 5E 31
Red Hill BA2: Cam 3E 41
Redland Pk. BA2: Bath 3A 16
(not continuous)
Redlands Ter. BA3: Mid N 5D 44
Redlynch La. BS31: Key 5A 6
RED POST 4H 41
Red Post Ct. BA2: Pea J 4H 41
Redwood Cl. BA3: Rads 5A 46
Redwoods, The BS31: Key 1C 6
Regal Ct. BA14: Trow 5D 30
Regents, The BS31: Key 1D 6
Regents Fld. BA2: Batham 1C 18

Regents Pl. BA14: Trow 1B 32
BA15: Brad A 5G 25
Regina, The BA1: Bath 2D 4
Reynold's Cl. BS31: Key 2F 7
Rhode Cl. BS31: Key 4F 7
Richardson Pl. BA2: C Down 2B 22
Richmond Cl. BA1: Bath 6G 11
BA14: Trow 6B 30
BS31: Key 3C 6
Richmond Hgts. BA1: Bath 5G 11
Richmond Hill BA1: Bath 6G 11
Richmond La. BA1: Bath 6G 11
Richmond Pl. BA1: Bath 6G 11
Richmond Rd. BA1: Bath 5G 11
Richmond Ter. BA1: Bath 6H 11
(off Claremont Bldgs.)
Rickfield BA15: Brad A 5E 25
Ridge, The BA15: Brad A 4H 25
Ridge Grn. Cl. BA2: Odd D 3E 21
Ringswell Gdns. BA1: Bath 6A 12
Ringwood Rd. BA2: Bath 3D 16
River Pl. BA2: Bath 3C 16
RIVERSIDE 6D 44
Riverside Cl. BA3: Mid N 6D 44
Riverside Cotts. BA3: Rads 3C 46
Riverside Ct. BA2: Bath 6C 4 (3G 17)
BA3: Mid N 6C 44
Riverside Gdns. BA1: Bath 5C 4
Riverside Rd. BA2: Bath 5B 4 (3F 17)
BA3: Mid N 6D 44
Riverside Wlk. BA3: Mid N 6D 44
(not continuous)
Rivers Rd. BA1: Bath 6H 11
(Claremont Bldgs.)
BA1: Bath 1G 17
(Mount Rd.)
Rivers St. BA1: Bath 2C 4 (2G 17)
Rivers St. M. BA1: Bath 2C 4 (2G 17)
Rivers St. Pl. BA1: Bath 2D 4
River Ter. BS31: Key 2E 7
Riverway BA14: Trow 4D 30
Riverway Ind. Pk. BA14: Trow 4D 30
Robin Cl. BA3: Mid N 5F 45
Rochfort Ct. BA2: Bath 1G 5 (1A 18)
Rochfort Pl. BA2: Bath 1F 5 (1H 17)
Rock Cotts. BA2: C Down 2A 22
Rock Hall Cotts. BA2: C Down 2A 22
Rock Hall La. BA2: C Down 2A 22
Rockhill Est. BS31: Key 3E 7
Rock La. BA2: C Down 5A 22
Rockliffe Av. BA2: Bath 1H 5 (1A 18)
Rockliffe Rd. BA2: Bath 1G 5 (1A 18)
Rock Rd. BA3: Mid N 3F 45
BA14: Trow 6C 30
BS31: Key 2D 6
Rodney Ho. BA2: Bath 3B 16
Rodney Rd. BS31: Salt 5B 8
Rodway Cl. BA14: Trow 3F 31
Rodwell Pk. BA14: Trow 3F 31
Rogers Cl. BS39: Clut 6A 36
Roman Baths 5E 5 (3H 17)
Roman Ho. BA1: Bath 1F 5
Roman Rd. BA2: Odd D, Eng 3D 20
Roman Way BA2: Pea J 4C 42
BS39: Paul 5E 39
Rondo Theatre, The 6B 12
Rooksbridge Wlk. BA2: Bath 3D 16
Ropewalk, The BA15: Brad A 5F 25
Roseberry Pl. BA2: Bath 3E 17
Roseberry Rd. BA2: Bath 3D 16
Rose Cotts. BA2: Odd D 3D 20
BA2: S'ske 4G 21
Rosedale Gdns. BA14: Trow 4B 30
Rose Hill BA1: Bath, Swa 5A 12
(not continuous)
Roseland Cl. BA1: Swa 4B 12
Rosemary Wlk. BA15: Brad A 4F 25
(off Newtown)
Rosemount La. BA2: Bath 5A 18
Rose Ter. BA2: C Down 1B 22
Rosewarn Cl. BA2: Bath 5B 16
Rosewell Ct. BA1: Bath 4C 4 (3G 17)

Rossett Gdns. BA14: Trow 5B 30
Rossini Cotts. BA1: Bath 1E 5
Rossiter Rd. BA2: Bath 6F 5 (4H 17)
Rosslyn Cl. BA1: Bath 2C 16
Rosslyn Rd. BA1: Bath 2C 16
ROTCOMBE 1F 39
Rotcombe La. BS39: High L 2F 39
Rotcombe Va. BS39: High L 1F 39
ROUND HILL 1C 46
Roundhill Gro. BA2: Bath 6C 16
Roundhill Pk. BA2: Bath 5B 16
Roundmoor Cl. BS31: Salt 4A 8
Roundstone St. BA14: Trow 4E 31
Rowacres BA2: Bath 6C 16
Rowan Ct. BA3: Rads 4H 45
Rowan Wlk. BS31: Key 3B 6
Rowden La. BA15: Brad A 1G 29
(not continuous)
Rowlands Cl. BA1: Bathf 5H 13
Royal Av. BA1: Bath 2B 4 (2F 17)
Royal Crescent 2B 4 (2F 17)
Royal Cres. BA1: Bath 2B 4 (2F 17)
ROYAL NATIONAL HOSPITAL FOR
RHEUMATIC DISEASES 4D 4 (3G 17)
Royal Photographic Society, The 5F 17
ROYAL UNITED HOSPITAL 1C 16
Rubens Cl. BS31: Key 2F 7
Rudgeway Rd. BS39: Paul 6G 39
Rudmore Pk. BA1: Bath 2B 16
Ruett La. BS39: Far G 1A 44
Rushey La. BA15: Brad L 1A 26
RUSH HILL 1D 20
Rush Hill BA2: Bath 1C 20
Ruskin Rd. BA3: Rads 4G 45
Russell St. BA1: Bath 2D 4 (2G 17)
Russetts, The BA14: Trow 6E 31
Russet Way BA2: Pea J 4B 42
Rutherford Ct. BA14: Trow 4E 31
(off Duke St.)
Rutland Cres. BA14: Trow 1D 32
Ryeland Way BA14: Trow 6F 31

S

Sabin Cl. BA2: Bath 6C 16
Saco Ho. BA1: Bath 5E 5
(off St James's Pde.)
Saffron Ct. BA1: Bath 1H 17
St Aldhelm Rd. BA15: Brad A 6H 25
St Andrews Ter. BA1: Bath 3D 4 (2G 17)
St Annes Av. BS31: Key 1C 6
St Annes Cl. BA14: S'wick 3B 32
St Anne's Ct. BS31: Key 1C 6
St Ann's Pl. BA1: Bath 4C 4
St Ann's Way BA2: Bath 4H 5 (3A 18)
St Anthony's Cl. BA3: Mid N 3E 45
St Augustines Rd. BA14: Trow 5C 30
St Barnabas Cl. BA3: Mid N 2F 45
St Cadoc Ho. BS31: Key 2E 7
St Catherine's Cl. BA2: Bath ...4H 5 (3B 18)
St Catherines Hospital BA1: Bath 5E 5
St Chad's Av. BA3: Mid N 4E 45
St Chad's Grn. BA3: Mid N 4E 45
St Charles Cl. BA3: Mid N 3E 45
St Christopher's Cl. BA2: Bath 2B 18
St Clement's Cl. BS31: Key 3D 6
St Clement's Rd. BS31: Key 2D 6
(not continuous)
St Dunstans Cl. BS31: Key 1D 6
St Francis Rd. BS31: Key 1B 6
St Georges Bldgs. BA1: Bath 3A 4
(off Up. Bristol Rd.)
St George's Hill BA2: Batham 1C 18
St Georges Pl. BA1: Bath 3B 4
(off Up. Bristol Rd.)
St Georges Rd. BS31: Key 1C 6
St Georges Ter. BA14: Trow 5D 30
St Georges Works BA14: Trow 5E 31
St James's Ct. BA14: Trow 4E 31
St James's Pde. BA1: Bath ...5D 5 (3G 17)
St James's Pk. BA1: Bath 1C 4 (1G 17)

St James's Pl. BA1: Bath 1C 4 (1G 17)
St James's Sq. BA1: Bath 1B 4 (1F 17)
St James's St. BA1: Bath 1C 4 (1G 17)
St John's BA1: Bath 1C 16
St John's Cl. BA2: Pea J 4H 41
St Johns Ct. BA2: Bath 2E 5 (2H 17)
　BS31: Key 1D 6
St John's Cres. BA3: Mid N 3E 45
　BA14: Trow 1A 32
St Johns Hospital BA1: Bath 5D 4
　(off Chapel Ct.)
St John's Pl. BA1: Bath 4D 4 (3G 17)
St Johns Rd. BA1: Bath 2D 16
　BA2: Bath 3E 5 (2H 17)
　BA2: Tim 2B 40
St Julian's Rd. BA2: Shos 1G 47
St Julien's Cl. BS39: Paul 1C 44
St Katherine's Quay BA15: Brad A ...6G 25
St Keyna Ct. BS31: Key 2E 7
St Keyna Rd. BS31: Key 2D 6
St Kilda's Rd. BA2: Bath 4E 17
St Ladoc Rd. BS31: Key 2C 6
St Laurence Rd. BA15: Brad A 6H 25
St Lawrence St. BA1: Bath 5E 5 (3H 17)
St Lukes Rd. BA2: Bath 6G 11
　BA3: Mid N 3D 44
St Margarets Cl. BA14: Trow 1B 32
　BS31: Key 1C 6
St Margaret's Ct. BA15: Brad A 5G 25
St Margaret's Hill BA15: Brad A 5G 25
St Margaret's Pl. BA15: Brad A 5G 25
St Margaret's Steps BA15: Brad A 5G 25
　(off St Margaret's Hill)
St Margaret's Vs. BA15: Brad A 5G 25
St Marks Cl. BS31: Key 1D 6
St Marks Gdns. BA2: Bath 6E 5 (4H 17)
St Mark's Rd. BA2: Bath 6E 5 (4H 17)
　BA3: Mid N 3E 45
St Martin's Ct. BA2: Odd D 2F 21
ST MARTIN'S HOSPITAL 2F 21
St Mary's Bldgs. BA2: Bath 6D 4 (4G 17)
St Mary's Cl. BA2: Bath 4H 5 (3A 18)
　BA2: Tim 1B 40
　BA14: Hilp 1F 31
St Mary's Gdns. BA14: Hilp 1F 31
St Mary's Grn. BA2: Tim 1B 40
St Marys Ri. BA3: Writ 3E 47
St Matthews Pl. BA2: Bath 6G 5 (4A 18)
St Michael's Cl. BA14: Hilp 2H 31
St Michaels Ct. BA2: Mon C 3D 22
St Michael's Pl. BA1: Bath 5D 4 (3G 17)
St Michael's Rd. BA1: Bath 2E 17
　BA2: Bath 4B 16
St Nicholas Cl. BA14: N Bra 4E 33
　BA15: W'ley 4A 24
St Nicholas Ct. BA2: Batham 6E 13
St Patrick's Ct. BA2: Bath 4H 5 (3A 18)
　BS31: Key 2D 6
St Pauls Pl. BA1: Bath 4C 4
　BA3: Mid N 3E 45
St Peter's Ct. BA2: Bath 3E 17
　(off Dorset Cl.)
St Peter's Pl. BA2: Bath 3E 17
St Peter's Rd. BA3: Mid N 5G 45
St Peter's Ter. BA2: Bath 5A 4 (3E 17)
St Saviours Rd. BA1: Bath, Swa ...6A 12
St Saviour's Ter. BA1: Bath 6A 12
St Saviours Way BA1: Bath 6B 12
St Stephen's Cl. BA1: Bath 6G 11
St Stephen's Ct. BA1: Bath 1G 17
St Stephen's Pl. BA1: Bath 1G 17
　BA14: Trow 5E 31
St Stephen's Rd. BA1: Bath 1D 4 (1G 17)
St Swithin's Pl. BA1: Bath 1E 5 (1H 17)
St Swithin's Yd. BA1: Bath 2E 5
St Thomas' Pas. BA14: Trow 4E 31
St Thomas Rd. BA3: Mid N 3F 45
　BA14: Trow 4E 31
St Winifred's Dr. BA2: C Down 1C 22
SALISBURY 1D 44
Salisbury Rd. BA1: Bath 5A 12
　BS39: Paul 1D 44

Salisbury Vw. BS39: Paul 1D 44
Sally Lunn's House 5E 5 (3H 17)
Salter Cl. BA14: Trow 6F 31
SALTFORD 4B 8
Saltford Ct. BS31: Salt 4B 8
Salway Cl. BS40: Chew S 4C 34
Sand Cl. BA15: Brad A 4H 25
Sanders Rd. BA14: Trow 3D 30
Sandford Pk. BA14: Trow 6A 30
Sandown Cen. BA14: Trow 3F 33
Sandringham Rd. BA14: Trow 2C 32
Sandy La. BS39: Stan D 2G 35
　BS40: Chew M, Stan D 2G 35
Sandy Leaze BA15: Brad A 5F 25
Saracen St. BA1: Bath 3E 5 (2H 17)
Saville Row BA1: Bath 2D 4 (2G 17)
Sawclose BA1: Bath 4D 4 (3G 17)
Saw Mills, The BA15: Brad A 1F 29
Saxon Dr. BA14: Trow 1F 31
Saxon Way BA2: Pea J 3C 42
　BA15: W'ley 4C 24
School La. BA1: Bathe 3E 13
　BA14: Stav 6E 27
　BA14: S'wick 4A 32
　BS39: Chelw 1C 36
　BS40: Chew S 5B 34
School La. Cl. BA14: Stav 6E 27
Scobell Ri. BS39: High L 1E 39
Scornfield La. BS40: Chew S 6B 34
Scot La. BS40: Chew S 4B 34
Scumbrum La. BS39: High L 6E 37
Second Av. BA2: Bath 5E 17
　BA3: Mid N 6G 45
Sedgemoor Rd. BA2: C Down 2G 21
Sedgemoor Ter. BA2: C Down 1H 21
Selbourne Cl. BA1: Bath 1B 16
Selway Ct. BA2: C Down 1A 22
Selworthy Cl. BS31: Key 2C 6
Selworthy Ho. BA2: C Down 1G 21
Selworthy Ter. BA2: C Down 1G 21
Seven Acres La. BA1: Bathe 2E 13
Seven Dials BA1: Bath 4D 4 (3G 17)
Severn Way BS31: Key 3E 7
Seward Ter. BA3: Writ 3E 47
Seymour Ct. BA14: Trow 4D 30
Seymour Rd. BA1: Bath 1H 17
　BA14: Trow 4D 30
Shaftesbury Av. BA1: Bath 2D 16
Shaftesbury Ct. BA14: Trow 1B 32
Shaftesbury M. BA2: Bath 4E 17
Shaftesbury Rd. BA2: Bath 6A 4 (4E 17)
Shaftesbury Ter. BA3: Rads 2C 46
Shaft Rd. BA2: C Down, Mon C 1C 22
Shails La. BA14: Trow 4D 30
Shails La. Ind. Est. BA14: Trow 4D 30
Shakespeare Av. BA2: Bath 5G 17
Shakespeare Rd. BA3: Rads 4G 45
Shallows, The BS31: Salt 4C 8
Shambles, The BA15: Brad A 6A 25
Sham Castle La. BA2: Bath 3H 5 (2A 18)
Shaws Way BA2: Bath 3A 16
Shearman St. BA14: Trow 6E 31
Sheepcote Barton BA14: Trow 6E 31
Shelley Rd. BA2: Bath 4G 17
　BA3: Rads 4G 45
Shepherd's Wlk. BA2: C Down 2G 21
Sheppards Gdns. BA1: W'ton 5C 10
Sherborne Rd. BA14: Trow 4A 30
Sheridan Gdns. BA14: Trow 1A 32
Sheridan Rd. BA2: Bath 4A 16
Sherwood Cl. BS31: Key 2D 6
Sherwood Rd. BS31: Key 2D 6
Shickle Gro. BA2: Odd D 2D 20
Shires, The BA14: Trow 5D 30
Shires Yd. BA1: Bath 3D 4 (2G 17)
Shockerwick La. BA1: Bathf, Sho 3G 13
Shophouse Rd. BA2: Bath 3C 16
Shop La. BA14: Wing 6F 29
Shoreditch BS40: Chew S 6A 34
Shore Pl. BA14: Trow 4A 30
SHOSCOMBE 5C 42
SHOSCOMBE VALE 6C 42

Shrewton Cl. BA14: Trow 1E 33
Shrubbery, The BA1: Bath 1C 4 (1G 17)
Shums Ct. BA1: Bath 4E 5
　(off Cheap St.)
Sidings, The BS39: Clut 6B 36
Silbury Ri. BS31: Key 5F 7
Silver Birch Gro. BA14: Trow 2C 32
Silver Mdws. BA14: Trow 2B 32
Silver St. BA3: Mid N, Stratt F 6E 45
　BA14: Trow 5E 31
　BA15: Brad A 5G 25
　BS40: Chew M 2F 35
Silver St. La. BA14: Trow 2B 32
Silver Thorne Barton BA14: Trow 4E 31
　(off Duke St.)
Simons Cl. BS39: Paul 6H 39
SINGLE HILL 6E 43
SION HILL 6F 11
Sion Hill BA1: Bath 6F 11
Sion Hill Pl. BA1: Bath 6F 11
Sion Pl. BA2: Bath 4H 5 (3A 18)
Sion Rd. BA1: Bath 6F 11
Sixpence BS39: High L 1F 39
Skinner's Hill BA2: Cam 4E 41
SLADEBROOK 6D 16
Sladebrook Av. BA2: Bath 6D 16
Sladebrook Ct. BA2: Bath 6C 16
Sladebrook Rd. BA2: Bath 5C 16
Slade Cotts. BA2: Mon C 2D 22
Sladesbrook BA15: Brad A 4G 25
Sladesbrook Cl. BA15: Brad A 3G 25
Sleightholme Ct. BA14: Trow 6D 30
Slipway, The BA14: Stav 1E 31
Slowgrove Cl. BA14: Trow 5G 31
Smallbrook Gdns. BA14: Stav 6E 27
Smallcombe Cl. BA3: Clan 6E 41
Smallcombe Rd. BA3: Clan 6E 41
Smallwood Vw. BA3: Mid N 6C 44
Smithywell Cl. BA14: Trow 5G 31
Snow Hill BA1: Bath 1H 17
Snow Hill Ho. BA1: Bath 1H 17
Solsbury Cl. BA1: Bathe 3E 13
　BA2: C'ton D 3E 19
Solsbury La. BA1: Bathe 3D 12
Solsbury Vw. BA2: Batham 6E 13
Solsbury Way BA1: Bath 5G 11
　(not continuous)
Somer Av. BA3: Mid N 3D 44
Somer Ct. BA3: Mid N 4F 45
SOMERDALE 1E 7
Somerdale Av. BA2: Odd D 1D 20
Somerdale Rd. BS31: Key 1E 7
Somerdale Vw. BA2: Bath 1D 20
Somer Ridge BA3: Mid N 2D 44
Somer Rd. BA3: Mid N 3D 44
Somerset & Dorset Railway Heritage Trust
　Midsomer Norton South Station ...5E 45
Somerset Folly BA2: Tim 1B 40
Somerset Ho. BA2: Bath 6E 17
Somerset La. BA1: Bath 6F 11
Somerset Pl. BA1: Bath 6F 11
Somerset St. BA1: Bath 6D 4 (4H 17)
Somerset Way BS39: Paul 5G 39
Somervale Rd. BA3: Rads 3A 46
Somerville Cl. BS31: Salt 5B 8
Sorrel Cl. BA14: Trow 2E 33
South Av. BA2: Bath 4E 17
Southbourne Gdns. BA1: Bath 6A 12
Southbourne Mans. BA2: Bath ...5F 5 (3H 17)
Southcot Pl. BA2: Bath 4H 17
SOUTH DOWN 6C 16
Southdown Av. BA2: Bath 6C 16
Southdown Rd. BA2: Bath 5C 16
SOUTHFIELD 3C 46
Southfield BA14: S'wick 5A 32
Southfield Ct. BA14: Trow 5F 31
Southfields BA3: Rads 3C 46
Southgate Pl. BA1: Bath 5E 5
Southgate Shop. Cen.
　BA1: Bath 6E 5 (4H 17)
Southgate St. BA1: Bath 5E 5 (3H 17)
　(not continuous)

Southlands BA1: W'ton 5B **10**
(not continuous)
Southlands Dr. BA2: Tim 2B **40**
Sth. Lea Rd. BA1: Bath 1B **16**
Southleigh BA15: Brad A 6F **25**
SOUTH LYNCOMBE **6G 17**
Southover Rd. BS39: High L 2F **39**
South Pde. BA2: Bath 5F **5** (3H **17**)
BS40: Chew M 2F **35**
South Pde. Cotts. *BA2: C Down 2B 22*
(off Tyning Rd.)
South Rd. BA2: Tim 2B **40**
BA3: Mid N 4E **45**
SOUTH STOKE **4G 21**
Southstoke La. BA2: S'ske 4G **21**
Southstoke Rd. BA2: C Down 2G **21**
SOUTH TWERTON **4E 17**
South Vw. *BA1: Bath 6H 11*
(off Camden Rd.)
BA2: C'ton D 1E **23**
BA2: Mon C 2D **22**
BA2: Tim 1B **40**
BA3: Clan 6E **41**
BS39: Paul .5G **39**
South Vw. Pl. BA2: Odd D 3D **20**
BA3: Mid N 3F **45**
South Vw. Rd. BA2: Bath 3E **17**
Southview Rd. BA14: Trow 1E **33**
Southville Cl. BA15: Brad A 6H **25**
Southville Rd. BA15: Brad A 6H **25**
Southville Ter. BA2: Bath 5A **18**
South Wansdyke Sports Cen. **4F 45**
Southway BA14: Trow 6E **31**
Southway Rd. BA15: Brad A 1G **29**
SOUTHWICK **4A 32**
Southwick Country Pk. **2A 32**
Southwick Rd. BA14: N Bra 5D **32**
Southwood Rd. BA14: Trow 5G **31**
Spa, The **2B 18**
Spa, The BA14: Holt 2F **27**
Space Health & Fitness **4G 17**
Spa La. BA1: Swa 5B **12**
Sparrow St. BA14: Trow 1F **33**
Spa Vis. Cen. **5D 4**
Specklemead BS39: Paul 6F **39**
Speedwell Cl. BA14: Trow 1E **33**
Spencer Dr. BA3: Mid N 3E **45**
Spencers Belle Vue BA1: Bath . . .1D **4** (1G **17**)
Spencers Orchard BA15: Brad A 6G **25**
Sperring Ct. BA3: Mid N 5D **44**
Spinners Cft. BA14: Trow 6E **31**
Spitfire Retail Pk., The
BA14: Trow 2E **33**
Spratts Bri. BS40: Chew M 2E **35**
Spring Cres. BA2: Bath 5F **5** (3H **17**)
Springfield BA2: Pea J 4A **42**
BA15: Brad A 5H **25**
Springfield Bldgs. BA3: Rads 2C **46**
Springfield Bungs. BS39: Paul 3B **44**
Springfield Cl. BA2: Bath 4C **16**
BA14: Trow 3F **31**
Springfield Crest BA3: Rads 2C **46**
Springfield Hgts. BA3: Clan 1A **46**
Springfield Pk. BA14: Trow 4F **31**
Springfield Pl. BA1: Bath 6G **11**
BA3: Clan 1A **46**
Spring Gdns. Rd. BA2: Bath 4F **5** (3H **17**)
(Argyle St.)
BA2: Bath 6F **5** (4H **17**)
(Ferry La.)
Spring Ground Rd. BS39: Paul 6G **39**
Springhill Cl. BS39: Paul 5E **39**
Spring La. BA1: Bath 5A **12**
Spring Mdws. BA14: Trow 2B **32**
Spring Va. BA1: Bath 5A **12**
Spruce Way BA2: Odd D 3F **21**
Square, The BA2: Bath 6C **4** (4G **17**)
BA2: Tim 1B **40**
BA2: Wel 2H **43**
BA14: Stav .5E **27**
BS39: Temp C 2A **38**
Stable Yd. BA2: Bath 3E **17**
Staddlestones BA3: Mid N 6D **44**
(not continuous)
Stallard St. BA14: Trow 5D **30**
Stall St. BA1: Bath 5E **5** (3H **17**)
STAMBRIDGE **4E 13**
Stambrook Pk. BA1: Bathe 2E **13**
Stancomb Av. BA14: Trow 4F **31**
Stanhope Pl. BA1: Bath 4B **4** (3F **17**)
Stanier Rd. BA1: Bath 3F **17**
BA2: Bath 4B **4** (3F **17**)
Stanley Ct. BA3: Mid N 3F **45**
Stanley Rd. W. BA2: Bath 4E **17**
Stanley Ter. BA3: Rads 2C **46**
Stanley Vs. *BA1: Bath 6H 11*
(off Camden Rd.)
Stanton Cl. BA14: Trow 2E **33**
STANTON PRIOR **6A 14**
Stanton Rd. BA2: Wel 2H **43**
BS40: Chew M 2F **35**
Stanway Cl. BA2: Odd D 2E **21**
Staple Gro. BS31: Key 2C **6**
Star, The BA14: Holt 3F **27**
Starfield Ct. BA14: Holt 3F **27**
Station App. BA14: Trow 5D **30**
BA15: Brad A 5F **25**
Station Ct. BA1: Bath 2D **16**
Station Rd. BA1: Bath 2D **16**
BA2: Batham 5E **13**
BA2: F'frd 6H **23**
BA3: Mid N .3F **45**
BA14: Holt .3F **27**
BS31: Key 1D **6**
BS39: Clut .6A **36**
STAVERTON **5E 27**
Staverton Rd. BA14: Holt 4E **27**
BA15: Brad A 3A **26**
Steam Mills BA3: Mid N 5D **44**
Steel Mills BS31: Key 3E **7**
Steway La. BA1: Bathe 2F **13**
STIDHAM **2H 7**
Stidham La. BS31: Key 1G **7**
Stillman Cl. BA14: Holt 3F **27**
Stirling Way BS31: Key 3D **6**
Stirtingale Av. BA2: Bath 6D **16**
Stirtingale Rd. BA2: Bath 6D **16**
Stockwood Hill BS31: Key 1B **6**
Stockwood La. BS14: Key 1A **6**
BS31: Key 1A **6**
STOCKWOOD VALE **1B 6**
Stockwood Va. BS31: Key 2A **6**
Stoke Hill BS40: Chew S 6B **34**
Stokehill BA14: Hilp 5H **31**
Stoke Mead BA2: Lim S 4E **23**
Stoneable Rd. BA3: Rads 2C **46**
Stoneage La. BA2: Pea J, Tun 1G **41**
Stonefield Cl. BA15: Brad A 6H **25**
Stonehouse Cl. BA2: C Down 1A **22**
Stonehouse La. BA2: C Down 1A **22**
Stoneleigh BS40: Chew M 2F **35**
Stoneleigh Ct. BA1: L'dwn 4F **11**
Stone Mills BA14: Trow 5D **30**
STONEY LITTLETON **5F 43**
Stoney Littleton Long Barrow **4H 43**
Stony La. BA2: New L 3H **15**
Stourton Pk. BA14: Hilp 5H **31**
Stowborough Cotts. *BA2: Pea J 3A 42*
(off Greenlands Rd.)
Stowey Rd. BS39: Bis S, Clut 1A **38**
Stratton Rd. BS31: Salt 4A **8**
Streamleaze BS40: Chew M 2F **35**
Streamside BS40: Chew M 2F **35**
Street, The BA2: F'boro 3H **37**
BA3: Rads 3B **46**
BA14: Holt 3E **27**
BS40: Chew S 5B **34**
SN12: B Gif .1H **27**
Stuart Cl. BA14: Trow 1F **31**
Stuart Pl. BA2: Bath 3E **17**
Studio, The **4D 4**
STUDLEY GREEN **1B 32**
Studley Ri. BA14: Trow 1E **33**
Sulis Mnr. Rd. BA2: Odd D 3D **20**
Sulis Sports Club **1D 22**
Summerdown Wlk. BA14: Trow 2D **32**
Summerfield Cotts. *BA1: Bath 6A 12*
(off Tyning La.)
Summerfield Rd. BA1: Bath 6H **11**
Summerfield Ter. BA1: Bath 6H **11**
Summerhayes BS39: Paul 1D **44**
Summerhill Rd. BA1: Bath 6E **11**
Summer La. BA2: C Down, Mon C 2A **22**
Summerlays Ct. BA2: Bath 5G **5** (3A **18**)
Summerlays Pl. BA2: Bath 5G **5**
Summerleaze BA14: Trow 1B **32**
BS31: Key 1D **6**
Sunderland St. BA2: Bath 3F **5** (2H **17**)
Sunnybank BA2: Bath 5A **18**
Sunnymead BA3: Mid N 3D **44**
BS31: Key 4E **7**
Sunnymount BA3: Mid N 3F **45**
Sunnyside BA2: S'ske 4G **21**
Sunnyside Vw. BA2: Pea J 4A **42**
Sunnyvale BA2: Cam 3E **41**
Sunridge Cl. BA3: Mid N 5D **44**
Sunridge Pk. BA3: Mid N 5D **44**
Sunset Cl. BA2: Pea J 4A **42**
Surrey Pl. BA14: Trow 6D **30**
Sussex Pl. BA2: Bath 6F **5** (4H **17**)
Sussex Wlk. BA14: Hilp 4G **31**
Sutcliffe Ho. BA1: Bath 1A **18**
Sutton St. BA2: Bath 2G **5** (2A **18**)
SWAINSWICK **2B 12**
Swainswick Gdns. BA1: Swa 5B **12**
Swainswick La. BA1: Swa 2B **12**
Swallow Cl. BA3: Mid N 5F **45**
Swallow Dr. BA14: Trow 5C **30**
Swallow St. BA1: Bath 5E **5** (3H **17**)
Swan Dr. BA14: Stav 6E **27**
Swift Dr. BA14: Trow 1F **33**
SWINEFORD **1D 8**
Sycamore Gro. BA14: Trow 1C **32**
Sycamore Rd. BA3: Rads 3D **46**
Sydenham Bldgs. BA2: Bath 6A **4** (4F **17**)
Sydenham Pl. *BA2: C Down 2B 22*
(off Tyning Rd.)
Sydenham Rd. BA2: Bath 5B **4** (3F **17**)
Sydenham Ter. BA2: C Down 2B **22**
Sydney Bldgs. BA2: Bath 4H **5** (3A **18**)
Sydney Ct. BA2: New L 4E **15**
Sydney Ho. BA2: Bath 2H **5**
Sydney M. BA2: Bath 3G **5** (2A **18**)
Sydney Pl. BA2: Bath 2G **5** (2A **18**)
Sydney Rd. BA2: Bath 3H **5** (2A **18**)
Sydney Wharf BA2: Bath 4H **5** (3A **18**)
Sylvester Dr. BA14: Hilp 4G **31**
Symes Pk. BA1: W'ton 5B **10**

T

Tadwick La. BA1: Up Swa 1H **11**
Talbot Rd. BA14: Trow 6B **30**
Tamar Dr. BS31: Key 3F **7**
Tamblyn Cl. BA3: Rads 2C **46**
Tamsin Ct. BS31: Key 2D **6**
Tamworth Rd. BS31: Key 3D **6**
Tanner Cl. BA3: Rads 5G **45**
Tanners Wlk. BA2: Bath 4A **16**
Tannery Ind. Est., The BA14: Holt 2E **27**
Taylor's Row BA15: Brad A 5G **25**
Taylors Vw. BA14: Trow 4E **31**
Teazle Ground Ct. BA14: Trow 4G **31**
Teddington Cl. BA2: Bath 5D **16**
Telford Ho. BA2: Bath 6E **17**
TEMPLE BRIDGE **4A 38**
TEMPLE CLOUD **2A 38**
Temple Ct. BA2: New L 4E **15**
BS31: Key 2D **6**
Temple Inn La. BS39: Temp C 2A **38**
Temple St. BS31: Key 2D **6**
Ten Acre Cotts. BA2: Ing 5A **20**
Tenantsfield La. BA3: Fox 1H **47**
Tenby Rd. BS31: Key 3C **6**
Tennis Ct. Av. BS39: Paul 6F **39**

Tenniscourt Cotts. BS39: Paul 6F **39**
Tennis Ct. Rd. BS39: Paul 6F **39**
Tennyson Cl. BS31: Key 1E **7**
Tennyson Pl. BA2: Bath 5G **17**
Tennyson Rd. BA1: Bath 2E **17**
Terrace Wlk. BA1: Bath 5E **5** (3H **17**)
Teviot Rd. BS31: Key 3F **7**
The . . . .
Names prefixed with 'The' for example 'The Academy' are indexed under the main name such as 'Academy, The'
Theatre Royal (Ustinov Studio)
Bath **4D 4**
Thermae Bath Spa . . . . **.5D 4**
Thestfield Dr. BA14: Stav 6D **26**
THICKET MEAD . . . . **.3D 44**
Third Av. BA2: Bath 4E **17**
BA3: Mid N .6H **45**
Thomas St. BA1: Bath 1F **5** (1H **17**)
Thornbank Gdns. BA2: Bath 6C **4** (4G **17**)
Thornbank Pl. BA2: Bath 6B **4** (4F **17**)
Ticket Mead BA3: Mid N 2D **44**
Tiledown BS39: Temp C 2B **38**
Tiledown Cl. BS39: Temp C 2B **38**
Tilley Cl. BA2: F'boro 3H **37**
BS31: Key 5F **7**
Tilley La. BA2: F'boro 4H **37**
Timbers, The BA3: Mid N 6F **45**
Timbrell St. BA14: Trow 4E **31**
TIMSBURY . . . . **.1B 40**
TIMSBURY BOTTOM . . . . **.2H 39**
Timsbury Ind. Est. BA2: Tim 6H **37**
Timsbury Rd. BS39: High L 2F **39**
Tintagel Cl. BS31: Key 2C **6**
Titan Barrow BA1: Bathf 5H **13**
Tithe Barn
Bradford-on-Avon . . . . **.6F 25**
Toll Bri. Rd. BA1: Bathe 4D **12**
Torridge Rd. BS31: Key 3F **7**
Tory BA15: Brad A 5F **25**
Tory Pl. BA15: Brad A 5F **25**
Total Fitness
Radstock . . . . **.2B 46**
Toucan St. BA14: Trow 1F **33**
Tourist Info. Cen.
Bath . . . . **.5E 5 (3H 17)**
Bradford-on-Avon . . . . **.5G 25**
Trowbridge . . . . **.5E 31**
Towcester Rd. BA14: Trow 3F **33**
Tower Cl. BA14: Trow 6B **30**
TOWNS END . . . . **.1C 44**
TOWNSEND . . . . **.5C 34**
Towpath Rd. BA14: Trow 1E **31**
Trafalgar Rd. BA1: W'ton 6C **10**
Tramshed, The BA1: Bath 3E **5** (2H **17**)
Treenwood Ind. Est. BA15: Brad A 1G **29**
Trenchard Rd. BS31: Salt 4A **8**
Trent Gro. BS31: Key 3F **7**
Trescothick Cl. BS31: Key 1C **6**
Triangle, The BS39: Paul 5G **39**
Triangle Ct. *BA2: Bath 4E* ***17***
(off Triangle Nth.)
Triangle E. BA2: Bath 4E **17**
Triangle Nth. BA2: Bath 3E **17**
Triangle Vs. BA2: Bath 4E **17**
Triangle W. BA2: Bath 4E **17**
Trim Bri. BA1: Bath 4D **4** (3G **17**)
Trim St. BA1: Bath 4D **4** (3G **17**)
Trinity Cl. BA1: Bath 5C **4** (3G **17**)
Trinity Pl. BA1: Bath 4C **4** (3G **17**)
Trinity Rd. BA2: C Down 1A **22**
Trinity St. BA1: Bath 5D **4** (3G **17**)
Trossachs Dr. BA2: Bath 1C **18**
TROWBRIDGE . . . . **.5E 31**
TROWBRIDGE COMMUNITY HOSPITAL
. . . . **.4D 30**
Trowbridge Ind. Est. BA14: Trow 2E **31**
Trowbridge Lodge Pk. BA14: Trow 5G **31**
Trowbridge Mus. . . . . **.5D 30**
Trowbridge Retail Pk. BA14: Trow 2E **33**
Trowbridge Rd. BA14: Hilp 3H **31**
BA15: Brad A 5G **25**
Trowbridge Sports Cen. . . . . **.1C 32**
Trowbridge Station (Rail) . . . . **.5D 30**
Trowle BA14: Trow 2B **30**
TROWLE COMMON . . . . **.3A 30**
Tudor Dr. BA14: Trow 1F **31**
Tun Bridge . . . . **.3F 35**
Tunbridge Cl. BS40: Chew M 3F **35**
Tunbridge Rd. BS40: Chew M 2F **35**
TUNLEY . . . . **.1G 41**
Tunley Hill BA2: Cam 1E **41**
TURLEIGH . . . . **.5C 24**
Turner Cl. BS31: Key 2F **7**
Turnstile Wlk. BA14: Trow 6D **30**
Twelve O'Clock La. BA2: New L 6E **15**
TWERTON . . . . **.4E 17**
Twerton Farm Cl. BA2: Bath 3C **16**
TWERTON HILL . . . . **.6B 16**
Twerton Pk. . . . . **.4C 16**
Twinhoe La. BA2: Wel 1H **43**
TYNING
BA2 . . . . **.1A 40**
BA3 . . . . **.2C 46**
Tyning, The BA2: Bath 6H **5** (4A **18**)
BA2: F'frd 6G **23**
Tyning Cl. BA14: Trow 6B **30**
Tyning End BA2: Bath 6H **5** (4A **18**)
Tyning Hill BA3: Rads 2C **46**
Tyning La. BA1: Bath 6A **12**
Tyning Pl. BA2: C Down 1B **22**
Tyning Rd. BA2: Batham 5E **13**
BA2: C Down 1B **22**
BA2: Pea J .4A **42**
BA15: W'ley 4B **24**
BS31: Salt 5B **8**
Tynings BS39: Clut 6A **36**
Tynings Way BA15: West 2C **28**
BS39: Clut 6A **36**
Tyning Ter. *BA1: Bath 6A* ***12***
(off Fairfield Rd.)

U

Ullswater Dr. BA1: Bath 5H **11**
Underhill Av. BA3: Mid N 3D **44**
Underhill La. BA3: Mid N 4B **44**
Under Knoll BA2: Pea J 2C **42**
Underleaf Way BA2: Pea J 4B **42**
Union Pas. BA1: Bath 4E **5** (3H **17**)
Union St. BA1: Bath 4E **5** (3H **17**)
BA14: Trow 4E **31**
Union Ter. BA2: Bath 6D **4**
Unity Ct. BS31: Key 2F **7**
Unity Rd. BS31: Key 2F **7**
(not continuous)
University of Bath . . . . **.4D 18**
University of Bath (Park & Ride) . . . . . **.3C 18**
University of Bath Sports Training Village
. . . . **.4E 19**
Uphill Dr. BA1: Bath 5A **12**
Uplands Cl. BA2: Lim S 4E **23**
Uplands Dr. BS31: Salt 5C **8**
Uplands Rd. BS31: Salt 5B **8**
Up. Bloomfield Rd. BA2: Odd D 3D **20**
Up. Borough Walls BA1: Bath . . .4D **4** (3G **17**)
Up. Bristol Rd. BA1: Bath 3A **4** (2D **16**)
BS39: Clut 5A **36**
Up. Broad St. BA14: Trow 4D **30**
Up. Broad St. Ct. *BA14: Trow 4D* ***30***
(off Manley Cl.)
Upper Bldgs. BA2: S'ske 4G **21**
Up. Camden Pl. BA1: Bath 1H **17**
Up. Church St. BA1: Bath 2C **4** (2G **17**)
Upper Ct. BA3: Mid N 5G **45**
Up. East Hayes BA1: Bath 6A **12**
Up. Hedgemead Rd.
BA1: Bath 1D **4** (1G **17**)
Up. Lambridge St. BA1: Bath 5B **12**
Up. Lansdown M. BA1: Bath 6G **11**
Upper Mill BA15: Brad A 5H **25**
Up. Oldfield Pk.
BA2: Bath . . . . .6A **4** & 6B **4** (4F **17**)
UPPER RADFORD . . . . **.3B 40**
Up. Regents Pk. BA15: Brad A 5G **25**
UPPER STUDLEY . . . . **.2B 32**
UPPER SWAINSWICK . . . . **.2A 12**
UPPER WESTON . . . . **.4C 10**
UPPER WESTWOOD . . . . **.1B 28**
Upper Westwood BA15: West 2A **28**

V

Vale Vw. BA3: Rads 3C **46**
Vale Vw. Pl. BA1: Bath 6A **12**
Vale Vw. Ter. BA1: Bathe 4E **13**
Valley Vw. BS39: Clut 6A **36**
Valley Vw. Cl. BA1: Bath 5A **12**
Valley Vw. Rd. BA1: Charl 4A **12**
BS39: Paul .5G **39**
Valley Wlk. BA3: Mid N 3F **45**
Van Diemen's La. BA1: L'dwn 5F **11**
Vandyck Av. BS31: Key 1E **7**
Vane St. BA2: Bath 3G **5** (2A **18**)
Vellore La. BA2: Bath 3H **5** (2A **18**)
Venus La. BS39: Clut 1A **38**
Vernham Gro. BA2: Odd D 2D **20**
Vernhamwood Cl. BA2: Odd D 2D **20**
Vernon Cl. BS31: Salt 4A **8**
Vernon Pk. BA2: Bath 3D **16**
Vernon Ter. BA2: Bath 3D **16**
Vernslade BA1: W'ton 5B **10**
Vicarage Gdns. BA2: Pea J 4H **41**
Victoria Art Gallery . . . . **.4E 5 (3H 17)**
Victoria Bri. Ct. BA1: Bath 3A **4**
Victoria Bri. Rd. BA1: Bath 3A **4** (3F **17**)
BA2: Bath 4A **4** (3F **17**)
Victoria Bldgs. BA2: Bath 4A **4** (3E **17**)
Victoria Cl. BA2: Bath 4D **16**
Victoria Gdns. BA1: Bathe 4E **13**
BA14: Trow 3F **31**
Victoria Ho. BA1: W'ton 1E **17**
Victoria Pk. Bus. Cen. BA1: Bath 2E **17**
Victoria Pl. *BA1: Bath 6B* ***12***
(off St Saviours Rd.)
BA2: C Down 2B **22**
BA2: S'ske .4G **21**
BS39: Paul .6F **39**
Victoria Rd. BA2: Bath 5A **4** (3E **17**)
BA14: Trow 2F **31**
BS31: Salt 4A **8**
Victoria Ter. BA2: Bath 3E **17**
BS39: Paul .5G **39**
VILLA FIELDS . . . . **.1A 18**
Vine Cotts. BA15: Brad A 5F **25**
Vinescroft BA14: Stav 6E **27**
Vineyards BA1: Bath 2E **5** (2H **17**)
Vivien Av. BA3: Mid N 3E **45**
Vulcan Ho. BA2: Bath 2F **5** (2H **17**)

W

Walcot Bldgs. BA1: Bath 1F **5** (1H **17**)
Walcot Ct. BA1: Bath 1F **5** (1H **17**)
Walcot Ga. BA1: Bath 1E **5** (1H **17**)
Walcot Ho. BA1: Bath 1H **17**
Walcot Pde. BA1: Bath 1E **5**
Walcot St. BA1: Bath 3E **5** (2H **17**)
Walcot Ter. BA1: Bath 1F **5** (1H **17**)
Waldegrave Rd. BA1: Bath 6F **11**
Waldegrave Ter. BA3: Rads 2C **46**
Walden Rd. BS31: Key 3F **7**
Waldrons Sq. *BA14: Trow 4D* ***30***
(off British Row)
Walk, The BA14: Holt 3E **27**
Wallace Rd. BA1: Bath 6A **12**
Wallenge Cl. BS39: Paul 5H **39**
Wallenge Dr. BS39: Paul 5G **39**
Walley La. BS40: Chew M, Chew S 5D **34**
Wally Ct. Rd. BS40: Chew S 5C **34**
Walmesley Chase BA14: Hilp 4G **31**
Walmsley Ter. *BA1: Bath 6A* ***12***
(off Snow Hill)

Walnut Bldgs. BA3: Rads 2C 46
Walnut Cl. BS31: Key 3B 6
Walnut Dr. BA2: Bath 5F 17
Walnut Gro. BA14: Trow 1C 32
Walnut Wlk. BS31: Key 3B 6
Waltining La. BA2: New L 3G 15
Walton Cl. BS31: Key 3C 6
Walwyn Cl. BA2: Bath 3B 16
Wansbeck Rd. BS31: Key 3F 7
Wansdyke Bus. Cen. BA2: Bath 5E 17
Wansdyke Rd. BA2: Odd D 2D 20
Wansdyke Workshops BA2: Pea J 4B 42
　BS31: Key 1F 7
Warbler Cl. BA14: Trow 5C 30
Warburton Cl. BA14: Trow 1B 32
WARLEIGH 4H 19
Warleigh Dr. BA1: Bathe 4F 13
Warleigh La. BA1: Warl .....1G 19 & 1A 24
Warminster Rd.
　BA2: Bath, Batham, C'ton ..2H 5 (1B 18)
　BA2: F'frd, Lim S, Mon C 6E 23
Warren Rd. BA14: Stav 6E 27
Warwick Gdns. BS39: Clut 6A 36
Warwick Rd. BA1: Bath 2C 16
　BS31: Key 3C 6
Warwick Vs. BA2: Bath 4D 16
Washpool La. BA2: Eng 1A 20
　BA2: Stan P 6B 14
Waterford Beck BA14: Trow 1A 32
Waterford Pk. BA3: Rads 5H 45
Waterfront Ho. BA2: Bath 6D 4 (4G 17)
Waterhouse La. BA2: Lim S 4D 22
Water La. BA3: Mid N 1E 45
Water Lily Cl. BA14: Stav 1D 30
Waterloo Bldgs. BA2: Bath 3C 16
　(not continuous)
Waterloo Rd. BA3: Rads 3B 46
Watermead Cl. BA1: Bath 5C 4
　(off Kingsmead W.)
WATERSIDE 4A 46
Waterside Ct. BA2: Bath 3D 16
Waterside Cres. BA3: Rads 4H 45
Waterside La. BA3: Kil 6B 46
Waterside Rd. BA3: Rads 4H 45
Waterside Way BA3: Rads 4H 45
Waterworks Rd. BA14: Trow 6C 30
Watery La. BA2: Bath 3B 16
　BS40: Winf 1A 34
Waveney Rd. BS31: Key 4F 7
Wayfield Gdns. BA1: Bathe 3E 13
Wayford Cl. BS31: Key 4F 7
Weal, The BA1: W'ton 5C 10
Weatherly Av. BA2: Odd D 1E 21
Weavers Dr. BA14: Trow 6E 31
Weavers Orchard BA2: Wel 2H 43
Webbers Ct. BA14: Trow 1B 32
Webbs Mead BS40: Chew S 5B 34
Wedgwood Rd. BA2: Bath 4A 16
Wedmore Cl. BA2: Bath 6B 16
Wedmore Pk. BA2: Bath 6B 16
Wedmore Rd. BS31: Salt 3A 8
Weekesley La. BA2: Cam 3C 40
Weir Cl. BS39: Paul 5G 39
Weirside Mill BA15: Brad A 5H 25
Welland Rd. BS31: Key 3E 7
Wellington Bldgs. BA1: W'ton 5C 10
WELLOW 2H 43
Wellow Brook Ct. BA3: Mid N 3F 45
Wellow Brook Mdw. BA3: Mid N 3F 45
Wellow La. BA2: Pea J 4H 41
　(not continuous)
Wellow Mead BA2: Pea J 4H 41
Wellow Rd. BA2: Pea J, Wel 4D 42
Wellow Tyning BA2: Pea J 4B 42
Well Path BA15: Brad A 5F 25
Wells Hill BA3: Rads 3B 46
Wells Rd. BA2: Bath 6C 4 (4F 17)
　BA2: Cor, New L 3B 14
　BA3: Rads 4G 45
　BS39: Hall 5C 38
　BS40: Chew M 1E 35
Wells Sq. BA3: Rads 3H 45

Wellsway BA2: Bath, Odd D 3E 21
　BA3: Rads 4H 45
　BS31: Key 2E 7
Wellsway Cl. BA2: Odd D 2E 21
Wellsway Pk. BA2: Odd D 3E 21
WELTON 3F 45
Welton Gro. BA3: Mid N 2E 45
WELTON HOLLOW 3H 45
Welton Rd. BA3: Rads 3A 46
Welton Va. BA3: Mid N 3F 45
Wesley Av. BA3: Rads 4G 45
Wesley Cl. BA14: S'wick 5A 32
Wesley La. BA14: S'wick 4A 32
Wesley Rd. BA14: Trow 6D 30
Wessex M. BA14: Trow 1E 33
W. Ashton Rd. BA14: Trow, W Ash 5F 31
Westacre Rd. BA3: Rads 4D 16
West Bath Riverside Path 3C 16
Westbourne Av. BS31: Key 2D 6
Westbourne Gdns. BA14: Trow 5C 30
Westbourne Ho. BA2: Bath 5F 5 (3H 17)
Westbourne M. BA14: Trow 5C 30
Westbourne Rd. BA14: Trow 5C 30
Westbrook Pk. BA1: W'ton 5B 10
Westbury Rd. BA14: Hey 5G 33
　BA14: Hey, N Bra, Yarn 4E 33
Westbury Ter. BA2: Dunk 6A 20
Westbury Vw. BA2: Pea J 3C 42
West Cl. BA2: Bath 4B 16
West Cotts. BA2: C Down 2B 22
Westcroft St. BA14: Trow 4D 30
Westdale Gdns. BA15: Brad A 5A 26
Westerleigh Rd. BA2: C Down 2A 22
WESTFIELD 4G 45
Westfield BA15: Brad A 4E 25
Westfield Cl. BA2: Bath 6F 17
　BA14: Trow 1B 32
　BS31: Key 2B 6
Westfield Ind. & Trad. Est.
　BA3: Mid N 5G 45
　(not continuous)
Westfield La. BS40: Chew M 1D 34
Westfield Pk. BA1: Bath 2B 16
Westfield Pk. Sth. BA1: Bath 2B 16
Westfield Rd. BA14: Trow 6B 30
Westfield Ter. BA3: Rads 4H 45
Westgate Bldgs. BA1: Bath 4D 4 (3G 17)
Westgate St. BA1: Bath 4D 4 (3G 17)
Westhall Rd. BA1: Bath 2E 17
WEST HILL GARDENS 4A 46
W. Hill Gdns. BA3: Rads 4H 45
　(not continuous)
W. Hill Rd. BA3: Rads 4H 45
W. Lea Rd. BA1: Bath 1B 16
Westmead Cotts. BA1: W'ton 5B 10
Westmead Cres. BA14: Trow 2C 32
Westmead Gdns. BA1: W'ton 5B 10
Westmoreland Dr. BA2: Bath ...5B 4 (3F 17)
Westmoreland Rd. BA2: Bath ...6B 4 (4F 17)
Westmoreland Sta. Rd.
　BA2: Bath 6B 4 (4F 17)
Westmoreland St. BA2: Bath ...6B 4 (4F 17)
WESTON 6C 10
Weston Farm La. BA1: W'ton 5C 10
Weston La. BA1: W'ton 6D 10
Weston Lock Retail BA2: Bath 3C 16
WESTON PARK 6D 10
Weston Pk. BA1: W'ton 6D 10
Weston Pk. Ct. BA1: W'ton 6E 11
Weston Pk. E. BA1: W'ton 1D 16
Weston Pk. W. BA1: W'ton 6D 10
Weston Rd. BA1: Bath, W'ton ...1A 4 (1E 17)
West Rd. BA3: Mid N 3E 45
West St. BA14: Trow 5D 30
　BA14: Stav 5G 21
Westview BS39: Paul 6E 39
Westview Orchard BA2: F'frd 6G 23
West Vw. Rd. BA1: Bathe 4F 13
　BS31: Key 2D 6
West Wilts Equestrian Cen. 1H 27
WESTWOOD 2C 28
Westwood BA2: C'ton D 3D 18

Westwood Av. BS39: High L 1E 39
Westwood Manor 2D 28
Westwood Rd. BA14: Trow 2F 29
　BA15: Brad A 2F 29
Westwoods BA1: Bathf 4G 13
Westwood Vw. BA2: Odd D 2D 20
Weymouth Ct. BA1: Bath 1G 5 (1A 18)
Weymouth St. BA1: Bath 1A 18
Whaddon La. BA14: Hilp 2H 31
Wheat Cl. BA14: Trow 6G 31
Wheathill Cl. BS31: Key 2B 6
Wheelers Cl. BA3: Mid N 3H 45
Wheelers Dr. BA3: Mid N 3G 45
WHEELER'S HILL 3G 45
Wheelers Rd. BA3: Mid N 3G 45
Whitebrook La. BA2: Pea J 3F 41
White City BA3: Mid N 2F 45
WHITE CROSS 5B 38
Whitefield Cl. BA1: Bathe 3G 13
White Hart Yd. BA14: Trow 5E 31
Whitehaven BA1: Bathf 1H 13
Whiteheads La. BA15: Brad A 4G 25
WHITE HILL 5D 42
White Hill BA2: Shos 6C 42
Whitehill BA15: Brad A 4G 25
White Horse Bus. Pk. BA14: Trow ...3F 33
White Horse Cl. BA14: Trow 1E 33
White Horse Rd. BA15: W'ley 4B 24
Whitelands Hill BA3: Rads 2D 46
Whitemore Ct. BA1: Bathe 3F 13
WHITE OX MEAD 2D 42
White Ox Mead La. BA2: Pea J 1D 42
White Row Hill BA14: Trow 2B 32
Whiterow Pk. BA14: Trow 1B 32
WHITEWAY 4A 16
Whiteway Rd. BA2: Bath 4H 15
WHITE WELLS 5A 12
Whitewells Rd. BA1: Bath 5H 11
Wicker Hill BA14: Trow 4D 30
Wick Ho. Cl. BS31: Salt 4A 8
WICKLANE 2F 41
Wick La. BA2: Cam 2F 41
WIDBROOK 2H 29
Widbrook Mdw. BA14: Trow 5B 30
Widbrook Vw. BA15: Brad A 6H 25
WIDCOMBE 6G 5 (4A 18)
Widcombe Cres. BA2: Bath 4A 18
Widcombe Hill
　BA2: Bath, C'ton D 6G 5 (4A 18)
Widcombe Pde. BA2: Bath 6F 5
Widcombe Ri. BA2: Bath 4A 18
Widcombe Ter. BA2: Bath 5A 18
Wilcot Cl. BA14: Trow 1D 32
Wilderness, The BA15: Brad A 4F 25
Williams Grn. BS39: Paul 5F 39
Williamstowe BA2: C Down 2B 22
William St. BA2: Bath 3F 5 (2H 17)
Willow Cl. BA2: Odd D 3E 21
　BA3: Rads 3A 46
Willow Falls, The BA1: Bathe 4D 12
Willow Grn. BA2: Bath 5F 17
Willow Gro. BA14: Trow 2C 32
Willows, The BS31: Key 1D 6
Willowside Pk. BA14: Trow 1E 31
Willow Vw. BA3: N Bra 4D 32
Willow Wlk. BS31: Key 3C 6
Wilton Dr. BA14: Trow 1E 33
Wiltshire Dr. BA14: Trow 2D 32
Wiltshire Music Cen. 4E 25
Wiltshire Way BA1: Bath 5H 11
Winchester Cl. BA14: N Bra 5D 32
Winchester Rd. BA2: Bath 6A 4 (4E 17)
Windermere Rd. BA14: Trow 3F 31
Windrush Cl. BA2: Bath 5A 16
Windrush Grn. BS31: Key 3F 7
Windrush Rd. BS31: Key 3F 7
Windsor Av. BS31: Key 3D 6
Windsor Bri. Rd. BA1: Bath 3E 17
　BA2: Bath 3E 17
Windsor Castle BA1: Bath 2E 17
　(off Up. Bristol Rd.)
Windsor Ct. BA1: Bath 2E 17

Windsor Dr. BA14: Trow 2C **32**
Windsor Pl. BA1: Bath 2D **16**
Windsor Rd. BA14: Trow 3F **33**
Windsor Ter. BS39: Paul 6G **39**
Windsor Vs. BA1: Bath 2D **16**
Windyridge BA15: West 2C **28**
Wine St. BA1: Bath 5E **5** (3H **17**)
   BA15: Brad A 4F **25**
Wine St. Ter. BA15: Brad A 5F **25**
Winford Rd. BS40: Chew M 2C **34**
WINGFIELD .6F **29**
Wingfield Rd. BA14: Trow 6B **30**
Winifred's La. BA1: Bath 6F **11**
Winscombe Cl. BS31: Key 1C **6**
WINSLEY 4B **24**
Winsley By-Pass BA15: W'ley 4A **24**
Winsley Hill BA2: Lim S 4F **23**
Winsley Rd. BA15: Brad A 4D **24**
WINTERFIELD 1C **44**
Winterfield Cl. BS39: Paul 1C **44**
Winterfield Pk. BS39: Paul 1C **44**
Winterfield Rd. BS39: Paul 6G **39**
Winterslow Rd. BA14: Trow 2C **32**
Wishford M. BA3: Mid N 3G **45**
Witham Rd. BS31: Key 4F **7**
Withies La. BA3: Mid N 6D **44**
Withies Pk. BA3: Mid N 6C **44**
Withy Cl. BA14: Trow 2F **31**
WITHY MILLS 4A **40**
Witney Cl. BS31: Salt 4A **8**
Woburn Cl. BA14: Trow 5B **30**
Woodborough Cl. BA14: Trow 2E **33**
WOODBOROUGH HILL 1E **47**
Woodborough La. BA3: Rads 1C **46**
Woodborough Rd. BA3: Rads 2C **46**

Woodford La. BS40: Chew S 5C **34**
Woodhill Pl. BA2: C'ton D 4C **18**
Woodhouse Gdns. BA14: Hilp 6H **31**
Woodhouse Rd. BA2: Bath 3B **16**
Woodland Gro. BA2: C'ton D 4D **18**
Woodland Pl. BA2: C'ton D 4C **18**
Woodlands Dr. BA2: Lim S 5G **23**
Woodlands Edge BA14: Trow 6G **31**
Woodlands Pk. BA1: Bath 5B **12**
Woodmand BA14: Holt 3G **27**
Woodmarsh BA14: N Bra 3E **33**
Woodpecker Av. BA3: Mid N 5F **45**
Woodpecker Dr. BA14: Trow 1F **33**
Woods Hill BA2: Lim S 5F **23**
Woodside BA3: Mid N 4C **44**
Woodside Cotts. BA2: Eng 3D **20**
Wood St. BA1: Bath 4D **4** (3G **17**)
   BA2: Bath 6C **4** (4G **17**)
Woodview BS39: Paul 6E **39**
Woodview Ter. BA2: Bath 3A **16**
WOOLLEY
   BA1 . . . . .1G **11**
   BA15 . . . . .4H **25**
Woolley Cl. BA15: Brad A 4H **25**
Woolley Dr. BA15: Brad A 4H **25**
WOOLLEY GREEN 3A **26**
Woolley La. BA1: Charl, W'ly 2G **11**
Woolley Orchard BA15: Brad A 4H **25**
Woolley St. BA15: Brad A 5G **25**
Woolley Ter. BA15: Brad A 4H **25**
Woolpack Mdws. BA14: Trow 6F **31**
Worcester Bldgs. BA1: Bath 5A **12**
Worcester Cl. BA2: Pea J 4B **42**
Worcester Ct. *BA1: Bath* *5A 12*
                  (off Worcester Pk.)

Worcester Pk. BA1: Bath 5A **12**
Worcester Pl. BA1: Bath 5A **12**
Worcester Ter. BA1: Bath 6A **12**
Worcester Vs. BA1: Bath 5A **12**
Worlds End La. BS31: Key 2H **7**
Worsted Cl. BA14: Trow 6F **31**
Wren Ct. BA14: Trow 5C **30**
WRITHLINGTON 3E **47**
Writhlington Ct. BA3: Writ 3D **46**
Writhlington Sports Cen. 4D **46**
Wyke Rd. BA14: Trow 6F **27**
Wynsome St. BA14: S'wick 4A **32**

Y

YARNBROOK 5G **33**
Yarnbrook Rd. BA14: W Ash, Yarn 4G **33**
Yarn Ter. BA14: Trow 6F **31**
Yeoman Way BA14: Trow 6D **30**
Yerbury St. BA14: Trow 4E **31**
Yew Ter. BA2: C'ton D 6E **19**
YMCA Health & Fitness Suite *3E 5*
                    (off Broad St Pl.)
Yomede Pk. BA1: Bath 2B **16**
York Bldgs. BA1: Bath 3D **4** (2G **17**)
   BA14: Trow 4E **31**
York Pl. BA1: Bath 1A **18**
York St. BA1: Bath 5E **5** (3H **17**)

Z

Zion Hill BA3: Clapt 6A **44**
ZION PLACE .6E **37**